Start Your Own Law Practice

A Guide to All the Things They Don't Teach in Law School about Starting Your Own Firm

by Judge William Huss

SPHINX® PUBLISHING
AN IMPRINT OF SOURCEBOOKS, INC.®
NAPERVILLE, ILLINOIS
www.SphinxLegal.com

First Edition: 2005

Published by: **Sphinx® Publishing, An Imprint of Sourcebooks, Inc.®**

Naperville Office
P.O. Box 4410
Naperville, Illinois 60567-4410
630-961-3900
Fax: 630-961-2168
www.sourcebooks.com
www.SphinxLegal.com

This publication is designed to provide accurate and authoritative information in regard to the subject matter covered. It is sold with the understanding that the publisher is not engaged in rendering legal, accounting, or other professional service. If legal advice or other expert assistance is required, the services of a competent professional person should be sought.

From a Declaration of Principles Jointly Adopted by a Committee of the American Bar Association and a Committee of Publishers and Associations

This product is not a substitute for legal advice.

Disclaimer required by Texas statutes.

Library of Congress Cataloging-in-Publication Data
Huss, William W.
  Start your own law practice : a guide to all the things they don't teach in law school about starting your own firm / by William Huss.-- 1st ed.
     p. cm.
  1. Solo law practice--United States. 2. Law offices--United States. I. Title.

KF300.H87 2005
340'.068--dc22

2005024650

Printed and bound in the United States of America.
RRD 10 9 8 7 6 5

*Dedicated to you, the lawyer,
devoted to creating something
that has never existed before—
your law firm.*

Acknowledgments

Volumes have been written on each subject in this book, and I owe a great debt to the many people who helped me found a law firm twenty-five years ago. The authors I studied for this book have my deepest gratitude for their help. A great many of my experiences in beginning my own firm are a part of this book. I am especially grateful for the collaboration of Stephen Acker in the section on office equipment, particularly computers and high-tech items. Steve has helped me advance into the IT world.

Special thanks go to Dianne Wheeler, former Division Manager of Sphinx Publishing, whose encouragement and support have helped me to articulate the purpose of this book.

Michael Bowen, Senior Legal Editor at Sphinx Publishing, is the inspiration for the ideas in this book. I am honored that he asked me to write it and helped me understand the vision and organization for it. His talent is invaluable.

Of the many who helped with putting this book together, I want to thank Janine Bronson, Betty Symank, and Mitch Cutler for their work in making my words understandable in written form.

The vital editing and organizing of the materials, without which there would be no book, was the result of the untiring efforts of a real genius, Judy Kleinberg—an author herself.

Behind all these efforts, especially my own, stands my wife, Marlene, who is an inspired organizer, team player, and leader. I am profoundly grateful to all mentioned here, but especially to her.

Contents

SECTION TWO: MANAGING YOUR LAW OFFICE

SECTION THREE: PERSONAL CONSIDERATIONS

Preface

There are many different ways of launching your legal career. Setting up a law practice is just one of them. Some of the other ways are touched upon in this book for comparative purposes, but the focus here is on the unique challenges of beginning your own practice.

Whether you are opening a solo practice right after law school or going off on your own after years of working in a firm, the information in this book helps you smooth out the bumps in the road to success. If you are joining others to set up a brand-new firm, it helps make your goals more attainable.

My hope is that this book reduces some of the stress of setting up your business so you can focus on the parts of the law that made you choose the profession in the first place. You have chosen a profession and worked hard to be successful. I want to honor your choice and your work by giving you a sensible, sophisticated guide that directs you to those who can help start your practice and provides suggestions so you can help yourself.

William Huss
2005

Section One:
Setting Up
Your Law Practice

chapter one

Finding the Right Location

Regardless of its size, your law practice is not only a business, but also a profession. Businesses need environments and procedures that are geared toward productivity and profitability. The things you do at the start of your practice and how you continue to conduct yourself and your business will have a direct impact on your success.

There is no absolute model for the structure of your practice. Within some general guidelines, it can be adapted to many variables—the number of lawyers, their individual needs, their geographical location, their finances, and all of the other factors that are involved in beginning a law practice. Each situation takes a lot of planning and creative thinking.

One of the first things you will need to consider in setting up your own practice is the location. A new law office that only has a post office box and an answering machine is not going to project the image of a successful enterprise. It may be very economical, but it is not effective in gaining new clients or reassuring existing clients. If your clients have difficulty contacting you, speaking to you, or leaving messages, you will have difficulty building a practice. Your new practice needs a home.

LOCATING YOUR PRACTICE

The location of your office space must be chosen with great care, while keeping your future in mind. Under most circumstances, the time you will spend at that location is going to be considerable—maybe your entire career.

Selecting the location for your law office is dependent on many factors. The location choice may depend on transportation (such as bus lines or subways), parking access, and other factors that make it convenient to clients and staff. Proximity to a courthouse may be a factor if you are planning on having a trial practice. Personal factors may also be a consideration. One lawyer took a map and a compass and drew a circle around his house, because he did not want to travel more than a certain distance from home to office. He located office buildings within that circle and found one that suited him. This arrangement was satisfactory for years. You must examine all the factors that are important to you and to the success of your practice, based on the needs of your clientele.

Before deciding on a specific location, you may need to decide in what type of community you wish to set up your practice. The size of your community—a small town, a medium-sized city, or a large, metropolitan area—can influence the location of your new practice.

Small Towns

In a small town, the cost of rent may be lower than in other areas, and clerical help may be available at lower salaries. Networking among members of a small community will probably be advantageous to someone who is from an established family in the community, went to school there, or has a net-work of relatives and friends as a source of clients. Someone who is new to the community may find it extremely difficult to compete with that kind of networking. Often, the initial contact between the client and the lawyer is quite likely to come from membership in local organizations and through personal referrals.

An important consideration for locating your practice in a small town is how far it may be from the primary court or county seat. The expense and time of travel for filing docu-ments, making court appearances, and conducting trials should be evaluated as you consider each location. In many instances, these are problems that can be resolved by having reciprocal counsel in the county seat to do these things. Obviously, this adds to the clients' costs, and in general, peo-ple in small towns have smaller incomes and are less willing to pay higher fees than people in medium-sized cities and metropolitan areas. Furthermore, the clientele in a small town is more likely to have legal matters that do not require large teams of lawyers and other personnel to handle.

A law office can be opened quite easily in a portion of the lawyer's residence when it is located in a small town. Law firms located in a lawyer's home or in a converted residence are found in medium-sized cities and metropolitan areas as well, but they usually are more likely to be economical in small towns. Small towns are less likely to have large office buildings, shared office suites, and other ways of establishing an office that may be more common in metropolitan areas and medium-sized cities. (The advantages and disadvantages of having your office space in your home will be dealt with in Chapter 4.)

The advantages of opening a law office in a small town include easy networking for the acquisition of clients, a more personally satisfying lifestyle, and potentially lower start-up costs. The disadvantages of a small town practice are isolation from the legal community of the county seat or main courthouse, transportation time and costs to that center, and difficulty obtaining critical business experience in order to maintain an economically viable practice.

Medium-Sized City

Beginning a practice in a medium-sized city can be quite satisfying, because it has the advantages of both a small town and a metropolitan area. It may be the county seat, but it may also have the advantage of local family and acquaintance networking for client development. There is often a supply of trained clerical help and other services, such as accountants and technical support.

The disadvantages of beginning a law practice in a medium-sized city are similar to those of a small town. For instance, there may not be a courthouse or a law library nearby. The economics of a law practice require that some research material be on hand, and the presence or absence of a law library can dictate how much money has to be invested to purchase your firm's own law library.

As in a small town, there may be only a few choices for office buildings (particularly office suites that can be shared), leaving the starting practitioner with fewer options. One option may be opening an office at home.

One of the most favorable characteristics of a medium-sized city for a lawyer is the availability of clubs and organizations that support the networking and referrals necessary to sustain a law practice. For example, a medium-sized city can support more than one golf club and other facilities that many attorneys use to entertain clientele. There are more—and larger—civic organizations to which a lawyer can belong and can help develop a practice.

A medium-sized city gives a lawyer an opportunity to establish a reputation and stand out in the community, whereas this may be more difficult in the metropolitan area. Like in a small town, a lawyer in a medium-sized city is able to become well-known relatively quickly, and thereby develop a client base more easily than in a metropolitan area.

Metropolitan Area

Beginning a law practice in a large metropolitan area has unique advantages and disadvantages. The advantages of a large city include the location of major courts and administrative bodies where the practice of law can be focused; large and easily accessible law libraries; a broad source of clients; and, easier client development due to the many ways of entertaining and meeting clients.

However, it is much more difficult to determine the competition for the kind of practice that you want to begin. The number of lawyers is so large that you will have to join the sections of the local bar associations that relate to your practice in order to get some idea of who the practitioners are in that area. Frequently, only a portion of lawyers are active in their specialty section, making assessment of competition even more difficult for the beginning law firm.

In large, metropolitan areas, wages and expenses are higher. Rent, insurance, and professional services—such as accountants, insurance brokers, bookkeepers, and other specialists—will be more costly. Fees attorneys charge are higher in the metropolitan setting in order to provide for these increased expenses. Consequently, the cash flow in a firm located in such an area has to be substantially higher than in a small town or medium-sized city.

Now that you have chosen the location of your practice, decide what kind of space you will need based upon your financial ability and your personal choices.

You will want to choose whether or not your office is going to be in your home or in a larger facility, and whether or not you are going to need room to expand.

The Goodwill of Your Location

The first location of your law practice is important, not only because it is expensive to have to relocate a short time after you open, but also because you begin to build a sort of goodwill with the location—your clients know where you are and how to get to you. There is a feeling of security that develops in your clients if they know that you are stable and easy to locate.

You want to choose your telephone number very carefully. You may want to even pay an extra charge to get a number that is easily remembered or spells out some kind of word that is identifiable with you or your practice. All of these things should be included in your budget after you inquire as to how much they cost. There is a great deal of goodwill in your phone number. It is printed on stationery and cards, and is found in other locations that people may keep for a long period of time. When people need you and are trying to call you, they cannot reach you if your number keeps changing. Ask your phone company about remote call-forwarding from your old number to your new one.

You should not have a post office box as your address, unless you absolutely cannot avoid it. When people see that as your address, they think you do not have a serious geographical location where you and your practice can be found. Deliveries are often more limited with post office boxes, and personal delivery by courier or otherwise cannot be made effectively to a post office box. If you have to use a post office box, arrange to have an address in an office suite where your mail and deliveries may be kept, and you can make arrangements to pick them up.

chapter two:
Structuring Your Practice

There are two primary means of opening a new law practice. One is as a sole practitioner; the other is as a duo-lawyer or multiple-lawyer practice. After you make that decision, you should determine the structure of your business. Depending on your needs and circumstances, your practice could be set up as a *sole proprietorship*, *partnership*, *corporation*, or one of the other limited liability forms of business now allowed in most states.

As you are deciding on how to structure your practice, it is helpful to reflect on your work habits both inside and outside of the practice of law. For example, have you been able to work alone on projects, get them organized, and take responsibility for their completion without involving the assistance of others? If so, then a sole practice might be easier for you than for those who work better as part of a team. If you examine your past activities and find that you work well with others and perhaps take leadership roles, then a multiple-member practice may be the place for you.

When developing the focus of a beginning law firm and its specialty, the overall philosophy for the law firm is a necessary ingredient in your planning. For example, consider whether or not the firm is going to include a certain portion of its work to be pro bono. Will the firm have a policy of seeking out handicapped employees? Will your firm be more than just a profit-making organization? All of these issues should be discussed among the beginning members of a firm, or considered in detail before the firm opens its doors.

The firm's goals are also important with respect to the initial planning. For example, a beginning firm might plan on increasing the number of lawyers in the firm on an annual basis, or developing a certain level of client base per year. These goals form the basis for the compensation allocation provisions of a partnership's governing documents.

SOLE PRACTITIONER

The sole practitioner approach is probably the most common, and in some ways, the most difficult. Sole practitioners have to be self-starters and self-organizers. They have the disadvantage of not having partners or associates available to discuss legal issues and get other opinions, which can be valuable in analyzing a legal problem. This is a good reason for sole practitioners to join a suite of lawyers or rent space from other lawyers, where they can easily exchange information during coffee breaks, lunch hours, and happy hours after work.

The various modes of practice have advantages and disadvantages. Some lawyers who work well alone and have a relatively narrow specialty find that a sole practice is best for them. Unfortunately, some sole practitioners do not specialize and want to handle any matter that comes through the door. This poses a danger to the lawyer and a disservice to both the clients and the legal system. In most jurisdictions, approximately 75% of all complaints made to bar associations with respect to lawyers and their practices are against sole or duo practitioners. Lawyers working alone seldom know enough about all of the subjects they are asked to handle, and mistakes are inevitable.

Sole practices also have a greater risk of encountering financial problems than larger firms. If just one client fails to meet his or her financial obligations, the firm may face a cash flow crisis that could terminate the practice if it goes on too long.

Sole practitioners may have difficulty handling large or complex cases, especially if there are multiple firms on the other side. Since this is where the large fees are made, being small is a decisive disadvantage.

For lawyers who are personally fulfilled by practicing alone, the advantages include the freedom of making all of the decisions, the freedom from wrangling over fees and distributions, and the personal satisfaction of achieving success by the use of their own wits. That sense of accomplishment is important and is a powerful motivation to those lawyers who work well alone. It helps them develop a practice and continue to succeed.

The sole practice is well-suited for small towns or suburban areas, where everyone tends to know everyone else, and the problems are rarely so catastrophic that a large firm has to be brought in. A sole practitioner can make a very good living taking care of small criminal cases, traffic and drunk driving matters, wills and probate matters, small business contracts, leases, and other services that fulfill people's needs in that kind of environment.

A solo lawyer who has an outside source of income—such as military retirement, early retirement, disability payments, or extra income from the family—may begin practice as a sole practitioner with the plan to expand the practice to include other lawyers in the future.

PARTNERSHIPS

You have to be brave to start a law practice, and it makes sense to want others around when you do. A partnership offers the advantages of having someone to brainstorm your cases with, share the expenses, and expand your database of clients. However, the main reason for entering a partnership is for financial gain. Partnerships typically generate a great deal more money than sole practices. The larger the law firm, the more likely it is that a practitioner will be handling large cases for large clients who generate large legal fees.

In a partnership, it is much easier to find an area that is fulfilling to you. Focus on that area, and specialize in it. Specialists tend to make more money than general practitioners, and by adding complementary specialists, the firm can grow toward a full-service operation.

When you start out with multiple lawyers, the task of finding an office location can be complicated by multiple viewpoints as to where the office should be located and what the cost of the expenses should be. Often, one of the beginning lawyers may be contributing less in terms of cash or financial support than the others.

Another problem is dividing up the labor of managing the firm, so that no one lawyer is burdened with non-billable time spent on management, while others are able to use their time more lucratively. The allocation of administrative and management functions is crucial, because if any one of them breaks down, the whole organization suffers.

Naturally, if you are a sole practitioner, all of the management functions fall upon your shoulders. When there are two or three lawyers, the management of the firm can be shared, or it can be done by one of the lawyers with an adjustment of compensation for the time that is taken to do non-billable activities.

Management includes such tasks as:
- hiring and firing employees;
- dealing with the bookkeeper to make sure bills are paid on time and that the financial management is not in disarray; and,
- making sure that the accounts receivable are monitored, as is critical to the financial success of the firm.

It is up to the lawyers in the firm to decide what management functions will be performed by each of them, or by one of them.

One way to ease the burden of imposing management functions on one of the lawyers is to have regular meetings of the members of the firm to discuss problems that arise. These problems may include difficult collection matters, difficult employee matters, and other things that the group should discuss before a decision is made on behalf of the firm. These meetings should be scheduled on a regular basis, such as every other week, and after hours, so that billable time is not consumed with such administrative things.

Checklist for Conducting Meetings

❏ Always have an agenda, even if it is a single-item meeting.

❏ Set a beginning and ending time, and begin precisely on time.

❏ One person must be in charge of the entire meeting, even though the management of the meeting may be delegated temporarily to others for reports and things of that kind. One person must always be perceived as being in charge.

❏ Make certain that every person at the meeting has an opportunity to ask questions, make comments, or contribute to the subject of the meeting.

❏ If someone attending the meeting is disruptive or causing problems, temporarily adjourn the meeting in order to cool tempers and deal with disruptive people. Once these matters are settled, the meeting can continue.

❏ If possible, keep written handouts to a minimum. The materials should be relatively easy to read and digest.

❏ If the meeting agenda deals with materials that have been distributed to the attendees before the meeting, all issues and questions pertaining to that material should be addressed in the time allotted for the meeting.

As the firm grows, it is advisable to hire an office administrator who is experienced in the structure of a law firm and the nature of the legal profession from a staff point of view. An experienced legal secretary can often be engaged for such work. Routine interviewing of new hires, performance evaluations, termination of employment, and things of that kind are often done by such administrators, so the lawyers can spend time creating revenue for the firm.

As the firm continues to grow, it will become necessary to have a partner devoted full-time to managing the firm. This becomes crucial after the firm increases to approximately fifteen lawyers. If you start your law firm with the plan that you are going to grow to the point where you reach that number of lawyers, you should include in your plan a requirement that one of the lawyers will have to become the managing partner.

Friendship and camaraderie are not sufficient bases for choosing the people who will help you begin your law practice. The ability for your partners to get along with each other is important. Their work habits, personal integrity, and ability to attract clients are crucial considerations. You must examine, among other things, their technical skills, people skills, and track record.

You may also want to find someone very different from you. Many duo practitioners are successful when one of them is more outgoing, gregarious, and feels comfortable with people, while the other is quiet, shy, and enjoys working alone. This can be a very effective working team. One does the legal research and the detailed deposition work, while the other does the client development and court appearances.

Partnership Agreement

Before a partnership is formed, the partners must discuss the plans for developing the practice, operating the office, and deciding who is responsible for the management functions. Partnerships can be formed orally or in writing, though an oral agreement may lead to problems down the road. In today's climate, a well-drafted partnership agreement is fundamental. However, lawyers who draft their own partnership agreements are inviting trouble. The partners should engage the services of a separate lawyer who specializes in such agreements, and pay the fee to get expert advice and well-drafted documents.

There are essential areas that should be covered in the agreement, such as capital contributions, profit sharing, and dissolution decisions regarding buy-and-sell agreements if one of the partners leaves. The partners must also establish standards for fee distribution within the firm, including the means of rewarding lawyers for bringing business to the firm, as well as the lawyers who actually work on cases.

One of the most important parts of a partnership agreement is the area devoted to the expansion of the partnership and how new partners shall be brought into the firm. Over the last fifty years, most large law practices have successfully expanded their client base through the acquisition of new lawyers.

LLP

Until recently, the standard partnership has traditionally been the most common form of law practice with multiple-lawyer firms. In such partnerships, the lawyers are entitled to an equal share of the income. They are also jointly liable for the liabilities of the partnership, putting their personal assets on the line. A *limited liability partnership* (LLP) is a way of protecting partners. A partner in an LLP has limited liability for the obligations of the partnership, or its liabilities to the partners or third parties.

In addition to uniform requirements, LLP determinations are established by the statutory or regulatory law of each jurisdiction. Each jurisdiction may have its own special requirements for insurance protection for professional liability and other protections for clients' interests. A lawyer may not avoid personal liability for the consequences of his or her professional errors and omissions, although jurisdictions may require maintaining malpractice insurance or allow the execution of a personal guarantee.

The downside to organizing and qualifying as an LLP becomes more apparent when it is time for the partnership to terminate or dissolve. There may be both state and federal tax problems. All of these considerations must be understood before the LLP is formed.

CORPORATIONS

The professional corporation is another form that the practice may take to protect you and other partners from liability. However, the primary advantage of the professional corporation is the establishment of pension and retirement plans.

Incorporating allows you to set aside pretax money for retirement funds. The money contributed to retirement plans is deducted when determining the corporation's taxable income. The tax on those funds upon the worker's retirement is probably going to be lower than the tax at the time the money is earned. Tax benefits also include the option of retaining earnings for a lower corporate income tax rate. The corporation's owning of automobiles and other large dollar items can also be a tax advantage for an individual.

Either a tax lawyer or a CPA should be consulted before making the decision to incorporate, because the financial implications are substantial. After consulting with a tax expert, you can decide more knowledgeably whether you should incorporate when you begin your practice. The advantages of incorporating are primarily financial and tax related, and would not generally be practical for a law firm that is just getting started.

There are differences of opinion as to the threshold for such a decision to incorporate, but there are two benchmarks to keep in mind.

1. If the individual lawyer's income is below $500,000, incorporation is impractical.
2. If the law firm has fewer than four principals, then incorporation is impractical.

Benefit Plans

Corporations have the option of establishing pension plans as well as profit-sharing plans, which allow contributions from profits if the board of directors so desires. You can maximize the options and flexibility of the corporation by adopting both plans. The secret to success of all these plans is the prudent adjustment of the money involved, and the added advantage that no income taxes are paid on those funds or their investment yields until the benefits are paid upon retirement or death.

The plans must be qualified under the applicable requirements of the Internal Revenue Service and the Department of Labor. While partnerships and sole practitioners can also receive similar tax deductions for retirement plans, the important difference is the maximum limits on such deductions.

One characteristic of these plans is that a corporation shall not discriminate in favor of the shareholders and must treat everyone equally. All employees must be covered under the

corporate and Keogh retirement plans, although the benefits and the coverage are variable based upon the annual compensation and length of service of each employee.

Other advantages of incorporation are the options of establishing medical and dental plans, which pay up to 100% of all employee and dependent care, either through insurance premiums or a fee for services. The corporation has an option of obtaining group term life insurance for each employee (currently up to about $50,000), and the premiums are deductible without causing taxable income to the employee or beneficiary of the policy. There are other options, such as sick pay and death and disability benefit plans, that the corporation may also obtain.

Transferring Ownership

One of the important advantages of incorporating that has very little to do with tax issues is the management of the transfer of shares when expanding the corporation. The shares can be issued by the corporation and bought and sold under limited circumstances by members of the corporation, and the relative monetary interest in the firm can be more easily identified and controlled. For example, the corporation may have a provision that the shares of the corporation can be sold only to those individuals who are invited or nominated to become shareholders in the firm by the firm's board of directors. This gives the firm the ability to determine with whom they are going to work and share their income.

This function is similar to that of a partnership, whereby one becomes a partner only when the other partners extend the invitation. That same personalized treatment is available even though the firm is incorporated. As the firm grows, this kind of procedure makes it a lot easier to bring in individual lawyers, or groups of lawyers, who are going to be added as a department to a firm.

Regardless of the mode or structure of the firm at the beginning, it is wise to prepare for the future and know what options you can have as you progress. If your plan is to remain a sole or dual practitioner or very small practice, you still need to have some long-range view for the future. If your plan is to grow, then the tax and nontax advantages of incorporating become more important as the firm expands.

Formalities of the Corporation

The formalities of incorporation are the same for all corporations. Corporate minutes and records of board meetings must be kept, and the separation of corporation issues and personal issues must be meticulously recorded. The corporation is the provider of the services—not the individual lawyer (although individual liability still applies).

Lawyers may not evade their professional and personal liability because they are incorporated. The corporation is the party to all of the firm's contracts, such as retainer agreements and contingency fee agreements.

There are other financial obligations of the corporation, such as annual fees, the added expense for administration of the pension plans, and the necessary tax deductions peculiar to the corporate mode. The Internal Revenue Service must recognize the corporation to allow all of the deductions to be taken, which is why the meticulous adherence to the rules is necessary.

The lawyers employed by the corporation should have written employment agreements, with the salaries and employment benefits specifically spelled out. The compensation for the principals must have some rational relationship to the services they render.

Professional Liability

As in a partnership, the principals in a professional corporation can be held to guarantee the liabilities of the others, within certain limits. A loan made to a corporation will almost always require the guarantee of one or more of the lawyers. The same is true for leases entered into by the corporation.

In a partnership, the partners may bear personal liability for things such as personal injury or property damage caused by an employee who is negligent or by a defective condition of the premises. In a corporation, the comprehensive general liability policy issued to the corporation should cover such liability without the maximum exposure of the individual lawyer's personal assets.

As with general partnerships, a professional corporation should have appropriate life insurance protection for the principals if one of them dies or becomes totally disabled. With the remaining principals as beneficiaries, the interest and the management of an enterprise is maintained within the confines of the firm.

Without such buy-and-sell agreements that protect the principals, intolerable problems could arise. When a principal dies without a provision protecting the remaining principals, the assets go to a nonlawyer beneficiary and the situation can become complicated. These situations can be handled easily with a properly drafted set of incorporating documents and appropriate insurance policies. These same problems can occur upon a marital dissolution.

FIRM AGREEMENTS

You or your partners may be beginning your own firm after leaving another law firm. If so, you must examine the employment contracts from the former firms, which may inhibit the establishment of a competing practice. In most jurisdictions, covenants not to compete are disfavored, but it does not mean they are absolutely unenforceable. It just means that they are enforceable only under certain circumstances.

For example, the partnership agreements for law firms may have provisions that govern the ability of firm partners or shareholders to be limited in their ability to compete with the firm itself. This does not apply to employed lawyers. This supports the strong public policy in favor of allowing clients to have the right to choose their attorney without being frustrated by restrictive agreements.

The different treatment of shareholders and partners is brought about because they have financial interests in the firm that they want to leave. The corporation or partnership has a right to determine who will receive that financial interest and try to make financial restrictions apply to its members.

Generally, these arrangements are negotiable, and mediation is one of the best ways to resolve disputes of corporate members and partners leaving their respective firms to practice elsewhere, even though it may be nearby.

CREATING A BUSINESS PLAN

Whatever you may envision for your law practice—sole practitioner, partnership, or multiple-lawyer office; urban or rural; corporate, personal injury, or other focus—the road map for reaching your goal lies in a well-executed business plan. Your business plan will not only help you steer your firm's development and keep it on track, but it will also assist you when you are seeking credit, applying for financing, taking on new lawyers, and managing your public image.

The most important reason for creating a business plan is that it motivates you to focus on the entirety of the scope of your business. It not only acts as a roadmap, but it also acts as a means of evaluating your strengths and weaknesses as a business owner.

For example, you may find that one of your strengths is the location of your office and its proximity to potential clients. You may also find that your weakness is an existing client base. You may want to reschedule the opening day of your offices until you have a client base that will support the renting or leasing of spaces, acquiring equipment, and hiring support staff.

Many of your important decisions can be made much more easily and intelligently when you develop your business plan early in your planning for starting your law practice. Your business plan defines the nature of your business, your customers, your resources, your competition, your short- and long-term financial projections, and your marketing. It should be built on specific and realistic terms—measurable objectives, identified responsibilities and deadlines, and practical budgets. Avoid hype, jargon, superlatives, and uncontrolled optimism when preparing your plan. Work toward a plan that is straightforward and simple, so it is easy to implement and easy to update as your business grows.

There are numerous books on how to write a business plan, some targeted specifically to the legal profession. You may also want to consider using one of the following software programs that will guide you step by step through the development of your plan.

- BizPlanBuilder from Jian: **www.jian.com**
- Business Plan Pro from Palo Alto Software: **www.paloalto.com**
- PlanMagic Business from Plan Magic Corporation: **http://planmagic.com**
- PlanWrite and PlanWrite Expert Edition from Business Resource Software, Inc.: **www.brs-inc.com**

However you approach the process, you will find that business plans have standard components. While this book cannot provide all of the details you will need to write a business plan, the following list gives a general idea of a typical plan's sections and scope.

- *Cover Sheet*: identifies your firm's name, the date, and your contact information.
- *Table of Contents.*
- *Executive Summary*: a single page that describes, in brief and simple terms, the highlights of your plan—the who, what, where, when, why, and how of your business.
- *Overview*: describes your practice in more detailed terms, including type of law, clients, location, physical office space, business structure, goals, general marketing approach, competition, strengths and weaknesses in the marketplace, operating procedures,

staff, insurance, and financial overview. Some of these topics are developed in further detail in the sections that follow.

- *In-Depth Financial Plan*: provides very specific and detailed information on business capitalization, including loans, credit resources, equipment, personnel, office improvement costs, deposits, and other start-up costs; balance sheet, with assets and liabilities; breakeven analysis; profit and loss statements; cash flow, including assumptions; write-offs; draws on income; and, accounting system. A three-year operating budget, including a detailed first-year analysis, with all rents, salaries, insurance, loans, taxes, and marketing, and quarterly budgets for the second and third years. Supporting documents, including copies of leases, licenses, partners' personal résumés, tax returns and financial statements, and other relevant documentation.

- *In-Depth Management Plan*: describes in very specific terms what skills you bring to the business, in addition to your knowledge of the law, and how you will manage and use staff to complement those skills and get the work done. Expands upon the information in your résumé, including your management experience, and identifies all staff tasks, responsibilities, resources, costs, benefits, and reporting and decision-making structures.

- *In-Depth Marketing Plan*: details who your clients are and how you will attract them, including all marketing and advertising strategies and associated budgets, sample materials, measurable goals and system for review, competition information, and specifics on how you will establish your pricing.

You might feel that you cannot write a business plan before you have a business, but you may be surprised at how many ideas you have once you start writing them down. These are the ideas that will help you create the practice you really want. As you begin to gather your thoughts and the necessary data, you may discover that your goals are unrealistic—or more in reach than you had anticipated.

It takes time to put together an effective business plan, so do not wait until your banker or future partner asks you for one. Take the time now to create a well-reasoned business plan to serve as an action plan that sets out your priorities—a checklist that will continue to guide your firm's growth even when you are successfully preoccupied with the business of law.

chapter three:
Business Formation Fundamentals

There are certain fundamental things that must be done in order for you to open your doors as a business—particularly as a professional office. This chapter provides a checklist that covers the start-up items that are easy to overlook. Some of the items on the checklist can be done simultaneously, and the order of importance can be changed somewhat to accommodate your circumstances. These fundamentals are listed to get you started.

IMPORTANT PRELIMINARIES

❏ Obtain your business license as the first act of your start-up. This will introduce you to the tax authorities for your locality, whether it be a city, a county, or both. You can expect them to come around within the first year or two of your operation to examine your premises to see if what you are reporting as income is probably true. You will need a license to start any business, and you must have an address. If you have not obtained premises yet,

you can use your home address. The business
address can be changed as many times as you like.

❏ You should register a fictitious name or a d/b/a
(doing business as), if your jurisdiction requires.
You can even put your name in the d/b/a, such as
The Law Offices of John Doe.

❏ Establish your office so that you have an address
and a place for your telephone. This is the time
when you should decide whether you want to
share space in a suite with others, obligate yourself
to a long-term lease, rent space on a month-to-
month basis, or start out in your home. Whatever
you decide to do, it is advisable to establish an
address that you plan to keep for at least two years
in order for you to develop a location in your
clients' minds.

❏ After deciding on your location and space, the next
thing that you want to do is to set up your telephone system. There are several long-distance
providers, and you should stay with a system that
is appropriate for the equipment that you can buy
from your local office supply source. You will need
at least a three-line phone with features, including
speakerphone, hold, mute, conferencing, and do-
not-disturb controls.

❏ If you plan to work on your computer or write
while you are on the telephone, you may want to
purchase an earloop that gives you a hands-free
option. *Office Rover* is a wireless loop that makes it
extremely convenient when you have to move
around while you are talking on the telephone. The

only problem may be incorporating its wireless feature into your regular telephone system.

❑ Your office will obviously need at least two lines, with the third line set up as a dedicated fax line that can be left open so the fax is available to your clients at all times. There is also a phone associated with the fax machine that gives you another line for outgoing calls if you need one. This eliminates your computer as a source of faxes and reduces the intrusion of outsiders into your computer system through that means.

❑ A telephone answering service can be very helpful when you are starting your practice. They can retrieve after-hours telephone calls for you, as well as cover for you when you are out of the office, when your staff is at lunch, or other times when you have no one to answer your phone. If your practice involves numerous individuals as clients, the expense of this kind of service is justified.

❑ Establish your email address and your website. Every professional office should have a website, and you will definitely need email.

❑ Your bank is your next stop. You want to set up your business account, your client trust account, and any other special bank accounts that you may need. For example, you may outsource the payroll function of your business to your bank, and there may be special accounts necessary for that. You should also open a safe-deposit box. If you are a corporation, you will need a resolution from the board of directors to do all of these things. If you are a partnership, you will need a signed order from the managing partner or one of the general partners to open such accounts. If you have obtained your assumed name certificate, it will be necessary for you to open your account in that name as well.

❏ You now have all of the information necessary to have your announcements, stationery, pleading papers, and business cards printed. Technically, it is possible to do all of these things with your computer; however, now is not the time to be stingy. You want to make a good impression and you want top quality printing on top quality stock for your announcements, stationery, pleading papers, and business cards. You may want to scan them into your system and print them up on lower quality paper later on, but in the beginning, you want to put your best foot forward. If your budget will allow it, you may want to have your business cards engraved. Some stationery companies will give you a special deal for a complete package of these items.

❏ Obtain the services of a reliable and qualified accountant, perhaps even a CPA, who will set up your accounting and bookkeeping system.

❏ Perhaps with the assistance of your accountant, obtain your federal tax identification number and any other tax related identification that your state may require (your accountant may have already done this for you). This may include an *Employer Identification Number* (EIN) and other things necessary to provide for the withholding requirements you will face as a business owner.

❏ Obtain the services of a knowledgeable insurance broker who will advise you as to the best policies for you, including comprehensive general liability, professional liability, unemployment compensation, and business interruption insurances. In certain areas there may be special need for flood, wind, or earthquake insurance coverage. All of these are quite expensive, and you should get some good insurance counseling on whether or not you need them.

❏ Obtain a credit card in the name of your business. This will help you in your bookkeeping for the charges you make for your firm. At the end of the year, a printout of the categories of your expenses can be quite helpful to you and your accountant.

❏ Apply for bar associations that are meaningful for you, including your state bar, the American Bar Association, your local county bar association, and any other specialty bar associations that will be helpful.

❏ Order local legal periodicals. Local legal newspapers can be quite expensive, and you must decide whether or not you want to incur that kind of expense in the beginning. If you are sharing offices, you may have access to such a newspaper without having to pay for it directly (but may be partially responsible through your monthly rental charges). If you are in a practice with more than one person, the cost can be divided. A sole practitioner may want to use the local courthouse library or county law library in order to read those periodicals without paying a high price.

❏ Set up the ability to accept credit cards. There are some clients, even business clients, who will want to pay for your services on a credit card. You will want to have the capacity to serve them. Here again, the credit card company can give you summaries of entries and categories of entries that will be helpful to you and your accountant.

OFFICE SPACE

Office space is one of the most important items to consider in beginning your law practice. Not only does office space constitute a major expense, but it also projects the image of who you are and what your firm is all about. Not only are these things important, but you and your staff will be working long hours nearly every day of the work week in this space. The feel and comfort of the space will directly affect your psychological and physical well-being.

While shopping for office space, it is wise to examine the area where you want to practice, and inquire of people who are already in that place or people who are offering office space to tell you the going rate for that particular space. This will give you an idea of what you may have to spend to be in that particular area. One of the best ways to do this is to get a broker to help you. A real estate broker's services are invaluable. They have the latest information on a particular market, the going rate of rents, and the amenities that are available.

If you decide that you want to pay a certain amount per square foot of office space and you want a certain number of square feet, then you have an idea of how much it's going to cost. You may then give the square foot requirement and the per square foot cost that you are willing to pay to a broker, and ask him or her to locate a space within the area you have chosen at that price. Let the broker loose to do his or her work, and quite often, he or she will come up with interesting deals.

Example

If your per square foot budget is somewhat low for that area, a broker may be able to work out a deal whereby you pay the going higher per square foot rate, but you get a certain number of free parking spaces. In some large cities, the parking costs are very high, and this can be an important consideration when you think about the net cost to you of renting an office without parking spaces and adding the cost of renting the parking spaces somewhere else separately.

Ask your broker to explain the details concerning your lease, if you decide to lease space. Lawyers are notorious when it comes to reading legal documents concerning their own affairs—they are either overly meticulous or do not read it at all. Whichever group you fall into, use the expertise of the broker to answer your questions and to become familiar with matters that you may not have dealt with before. For example, some leases alleviate the responsibilities of the lessor for maintenance, repairs, and other things that could be of substantial expense in the future.

Further, if this is your first experience with a commercial lease or if you are unfamiliar with this particular geographic area, discuss with your broker all the important aspects of leasing. For example, rents may be very stable, going up, or coming down. Discuss comparable facilities and their annual rates in order for you to have a good understanding of how much you should pay. Specifically, discuss the following things with your broker, as well as anything else pertinent to your situation.

- The length of the lease determined by whether rents are going up or going down;
- The cost per square foot;
- Additional considerations, such as parking or parking validations provided by the lessor as a part of the lease;
- The amount of the security deposit; and,
- The first and last months' rent deposit requirement.

Negotiating the Lease

Each of the foregoing considerations must be included in the negotiations for the terms of the lease. If you are in a position to bargain—for example, when the market is a buyers' market—then you want to press hard for lower per square foot cost, more complimentary parking spaces or validations, and lower security deposits. One of the factors to negotiate is whether or not last month's rent should be in the full amount. Some landlords are willing to negotiate this figure. You may be able to pay the last month's rent over the initial portion of the lease until it is satisfied.

You should think seriously about whether or not you want to expand your law practice and include other lawyers in the future. If you are going to expand, then you should include in your negotiations for the lease the option to lease additional space, either contiguous to yours or somewhere in the facility, at the rate that you are paying at the time you exercise the option. You may even want to include the right of first refusal to a certain number of square feet that are contiguous to your space, if that area becomes available, for you to exercise your option to lease.

It is not a simple matter to determine the square foot require-ment for you to start work. The basic minimum square foot space should include an area for a small waiting room, an area for your staff (even it is only one person), a small con-ference room, and your office. The minimum for a sole prac-titioner is about 1,500 square feet. This minimum amount can be expanded, depending upon your needs and the local costs as they relate to your budget.

All of the specific areas in the office can be contracted or expanded, depending on your budget and your type of prac-tice. If your clients rarely come to your office, you may not need the space for a waiting room and may need only the conference room. If you plan to expand and you want to include one or more office spaces, the conference room and waiting area may not need to be expanded at all beyond what you need for one office.

If you wish to expand in the future, it is important to choose your office space in such a way that you can expand in the spaces near you or somewhere else in the building. If you have no plans to expand your personnel, your choices are much easier to make. If you plan to expand and the building that you like does not have the capacity to accommodate your future expansion, this will affect your decision as to the length of your lease.

Leasing Alternatives

Renting space rather than leasing space gives you the flexibil-ity that you may need in this situation. When you are renting, you may leave much faster (usually within thirty days), but the landlord can also ask you to leave on such short notice. The flexibility in renting may be what you want when you are starting out and your plans for expansion depend on many variables, such as the number of clients you are able to acquire in a short time.

The possibility of having to move and lose the goodwill you developed at a certain location is a great disadvantage, and should be a prime consideration in your decision whether to rent or lease. There are other considerations, of course, such as your telephone number, stationery, business cards, pleading papers, and other things with your address on them. You do not want to send a signal to your clients that you move around a lot, which may make them think that you are an unstable practitioner.

Since the expense of starting your own practice can be great, you may want to use shared office space. You can have the large equipment expense included in your monthly charge, rather than having to decide, initially, whether to lease or buy, or hire full- or part-time staff. The time spent on shopping for equipment and furniture, and interviewing and hiring staff, may be better spent in developing clients or devoted to the work that you have to do in order to increase your client base and client satisfaction.

chapter four:
Your Office at Home

The first thing learned by a lawyer working for a firm is the billable hour. It is the standard for the legal profession, and many firms require a minimum of between 2000 and 2500 billable hours annually. The time that the young lawyer has for family, pro bono work, and community activities is severely limited—if there is any time for those activities at all. This kind of pressure for billing is not limited to beginning associates—it also can affect junior partners and senior partners in large firms, particularly in metropolitan areas.

This motivates a lot of practitioners to look for alternatives to the minimum billable hour mandate. One of those alternatives is to have your office in your home. This is quite often a very good alternative in a small town or even in a small city. This kind of alternative is available even in large, metropolitan areas, although very rare. The difference between the small town and the other locations is often perception. In a large city, the competition is usually in an office building, which has the effect on clients of projecting the image that the lawyer with a home office is outside the norm, and is possibly struggling to succeed. A potential client may seek someone who is perceived to be more successful.

On the other hand, having your law practice in your home can be extremely valuable to those clients who want to have an on-going, personal relationship with their lawyer. This can occur even in the business world, where general counsel and other executives in the company feel comfortable with their lawyer having a close relationship with them and a hands-on knowledge of the client's company or business.

THE HOME OFFICE ADVANTAGE

It has been estimated that of the approximately one million lawyers in the United States, about 40% would rather be doing something other than practicing law. This level of dissatisfaction cannot be attributed to the stresses of the billable hour alone, but such stresses are a major factor in the dissatisfaction expressed by many lawyers. One way to reduce these stresses is to have your practice in your home. This way, you can personalize your relationship with clients and have more time for activities outside of the practice, creating a higher level of satisfaction for you as an individual.

As more and more businesses use alternative work locations and incorporate them into their daily practices, the greater the general acceptance will be. It has been estimated that almost thirty-eight million people work out of their homes, and approximately ten million of those people work out of their homes full-time. Telecommuting is increasingly becoming a preferred style of conducting business. This will permit home-based offices to increase in business and in individual professions.

THE HOME OFFICE CHALLENGE

Starting your office in any of the locations discussed is a daunting task, and setting up an office in your home has its own set of challenges. The issue of separation of personal space from professional space is critical. The floor plan of your home must be compatible with accommodating an office space for you. There has to be the necessary security and privacy of client's files and information. Your clients have to know that their work is secure and not exposed to the casual prying eye of outsiders.

Other challenges exist that are particularly specific to the home office. One such challenge is the problem of zoning restrictions for the area where your home is located. Think of how embarrassing and costly it would be to change your office from your home to some other location because the neighbors complained to the authorities that you are in violation of a zoning restriction you failed to learn about. There are certain basic questions that you should consider before opening your office in your home.

- Are clients willing to accept your office in your home?
- Have you checked the zoning restrictions?
- Is it physically possible to separate the home area from the office area?
- Can you provide security and privacy for your workspace?
- Have you established a backup for when you are on vacation or otherwise engaged and need coverage for court?

Clearly, the physical location of your office can be critical to your law practice—especially when you are starting out.

Your address and telephone number become identified with you by your clients and colleagues. It is important to consider how long you plan to be at a certain location, because you do not want to make too many changes.

However, making changes can send signals to others, and you can take good advantage of them when promoting and marketing your law firm. For example, if you move from a firm of many lawyers to your home office, it can send the signal that you are not only starting your own law firm, but also that you are going to give very personal service, which most clients want from their attorney. On the other hand, if you move from your home office to an office building or to a firm with other lawyers, you may be indicating that you are moving up in the world and can give your clients broader services.

If you stay in one location for a long time, you may be indicting that you are stable and reliable, which is also very good for your clients. Whatever you do in your law practice, location is an important aspect of your marketing. Perception of you by others can become the reality of their view of you, so work carefully on what they perceive about you.

chapter five:
Office Design, Layout, and Furnishings

Once your location is selected, you want to look at the office with an eye toward utility and aesthetics. Furnishing your office with antiques, oriental rugs, and expensive oil paintings may be your goal, but such capital outlay can be substantial and far more than is necessary for your purposes. Simple furniture and carpeting is quite acceptable for most practices. Whatever your style choices, furniture should be cared for, comfortable, and practical for long hours of sitting.

DÉCOR

You may wish to get expert advice from an interior decorator. A well thought out color scheme and the appropriate placement of furniture can transform a relatively plain law firm into a pleasant, charming, and relaxing place for you, your staff, and your clients.

If you cannot afford a decorator, there are other ways of getting such help. For example, if you buy furniture or accessories from department stores, you can take advantage of their free decorator services. Having a family member as your decorator should be avoided, if possible, because it is difficult to tell the family member what you really want in décor. This can be the issue of a great deal of debate and dispute, and you should avoid that when you are just beginning. Sometimes it cannot be helped, and your spouse, in-laws, or other relatives will volunteer to help you with your office design and décor. The positive side of this is that the expense may be less than if you hire a professional.

If you are going to be setting up your office in a shared office suite, the furniture will often be provided, with charges included in the monthly rent. One of the advantages of a shared office space at the beginning of your law practice is that the work of professional decorators is clearly visible. A shared suite is a relatively large area to design and it generates enough profit to pay a professional designer to make the place look outstanding.

Your overall décor may also be affected by the type of practice you have. The firm that is principally an insurance law practice will find that the clients rarely come to the office, and the use of expensive decorations is not necessary. On the other hand, there are corporate clients who expect a lawyer not only to be successful, but also to look that way—expensive fixtures are expected and enjoyed.

The overall attitude of people who work in the office will be affected by the color scheme, quality of the furniture, decorations, and other aspects of the office. Sculptures and paintings that are done by someone connected with the firm can be excellent conversation pieces. However, keep in mind that if you put one relative's artwork in your office and not another's, you may have a family problem. Another way of making your office attractive and appealing is to choose an artist whose work you would like to collect. You may be able to obtain pieces of art at relatively low prices from an artist who is also beginning a professional life.

Lawyers and staff should be given the opportunity to display some items that are unique to them as a part of their office décor. This should be done with reasonable limitations, assuring, for example, that overgrown plants do not intrude on adjacent spaces, and areas that are visible to clients are kept uncluttered and consistent with the office design scheme. (Once your practice is established, you may want to hire a plant maintenance service to assure that all office flora stays healthy and attractive.)

The limitation on personal decorations should be explained at the outset, so that people are not embarrassed to discover that their décor has caused a problem. Such personal issues can demand unusual tact and diplomacy.

WORKSPACE PLANNING

The physical workspace must be organized or it will be difficult to get a clear view of what the priorities are, leading to a very stressful and unproductive environment. If the things that you use most are not within arm's reach, you tend to create piles and increase your stress level.

Having the right kind of furniture and placing the furniture properly is essential in running a smooth office. For example, a four-drawer lateral file is useful if the room is long and narrow, and it will work much better than a regular four-drawer filing cabinet that extends out to the middle of the room. This will afford you more walking space in the office.

The most efficient workspace configuration is that of the "U" shape. The desk, computer, and counter or credenza area form this shape. To avoid interruptions, try to avoid sitting directly in front of a doorway. Rearrange the furniture or have a tall plant properly placed to avoid a direct visual line of sight to you when at your desk. At the same time, avoid at all costs having your back to the office door.

Items that you use daily should be within arm's reach and everything else should be put away. A simple exercise can be used to determine which items are used daily and which are in easy reach. Sit in your chair, stretch out your arms, and rotate slowly around in the swivel chair. This will help you determine what items are within easy reach, such as the telephone, stapler, tape dispenser, calendar, computer keyboard, and other necessary supplies.

The furniture configuration should allow you to stand up during the day and take some in-place exercises, because sitting all day is not healthy. This use of space is also important when you want to stand while you are talking either to a person in your office or on the telephone. By standing during such conversations, you can keep them shorter and ultimately get more work done.

The lawyer's office should be a pleasant place to work, suitable for long hours. In many law offices in large buildings, the need to economize space has mandated that lawyers have very small offices, furnished with little more than a desk, a chair, and two clients' chairs. A small table to hold flowers and pictures can make even a very small office more attrac-

tive. Typically, senior partners have larger offices or corner offices. These larger offices clearly convey the prestige of the person who is occupying them, and this is not lost on clients and other lawyers who visit the office.

Lawyer's Office Checklist

❏ Desk approximately six feet wide with non-scratch and spill-proof surface

❏ High-backed chair with wheels or rollers to move about

❏ Two to four comfortable chairs for clients

❏ Large clear floor pad for chair in carpeted office

❏ Floor lamp

❏ Live plants

❏ Photo of family

❏ Wastebasket

❏ Table or special desk for computer

❏ Bookshelves

❏ Framed diplomas and awards

❏ Favorite pictures

THE WAITING ROOM

Various parts of law offices require different kinds of furniture. The waiting room is the first thing that people see. The statement made by the décor and furniture of the waiting room is very important, and should not look cheap or skimpy. While you do not want your clients to think that they are paying for opulent offices, you want to convey a subtle message of solid success.

The reception area should have comfortable seating for about five people. It is more expensive to use all chairs rather than a couch or two, but people in the waiting room will be more comfortable in individual chairs. You should also provide a coffee table or side tables with magazines and other reading materials so that people have something to focus on while they are waiting for their appointment. The reception area offers an excellent opportunity to establish the image of the firm quickly without extravagant cost. A painting or two, and perhaps some decorative fabric or small sculptures, will set a tone of tasteful professionalism that will help your visitors feel at ease.

Basic Reception Room Checklist

❏ Five comfortable chairs
❏ Hat and coat rack
❏ Umbrella stand
❏ Coffee table
❏ Reading light
❏ Magazine rack
❏ Telephone
❏ Side table
❏ Live plants

SUPPORT STAFF AREA

The area for secretaries, clerks, support personnel, book-keepers, legal assistants, paralegals, and other assistants should be separate from the public areas and utility rooms, to promote efficient work, preserve confidentiality, and mini-mize overheard conversations. Secretaries' desks should be located as close as possible to the lawyers with whom they work. Office furniture stores or your decorator will help you determine what furniture you should use in the secretarial area, but you should have a basic desk with a return, computer, telephone, chair, and shelves.

Basic Secretarial Area Checklist

❏ Secretarial desk, with a return for a typewriter and a computer
❏ Secretarial chair
❏ Roller pad for carpeted area
❏ Storage space for forms and supplies

COMMON SPACES

Lighting throughout the office should be both general and task-specific. Arrange lighting to minimize glare and reflections on computer monitors. Lower light levels in hallways can be offset with spotlighting on artwork. To reduce electricity costs, you may want to install motion detector on/off switches in rooms that are not occupied full-time, such as storage areas and restrooms.

Noise control is critical in law offices. Conversations and equipment sounds can travel throughout the office and disturb everyone within earshot. Carpeting is very effective in muffling sound, and fabric-covered walls or work station dividers also help reduce noise. You may want to establish an office policy about the use of hands-free phones, radios, other personal electronic sound equipment, and sound levels on office computers.

Somewhere in the office there should be storage facilities for legal forms, stationery, and office supplies. Often, this is kept in the file room of beginning law firms.

An employee lounge gives those who share the office a place to socialize and communicate within the workplace without disturbing coworkers. This can be extremely valuable in maintaining high morale. The furniture and décor of the kitchen or lounge area is usually quite simple and straightforward. Consider the needs of staff, clients, and other visitors in outfitting the kitchen. Coffee equipment, soft drink dispensers, and refrigerators should be adequate to support staff needs and to provide for serving office guests. You may wish to purchase a set of china cups for serving coffee to clients.

Whether or not the firm is going to make snacks available at the firm's expense or at the employee's expense is a determination to be made at the outset. Regardless of the size of the firm, there are companies that provide coffee service, snack service, catering for lunches and coffee breaks, and other amenities. This may mean that the firm does not have to maintain equipment and supplies to provide for its personnel. This is particularly valuable for small firms.

Employee Lounge Checklist

❏ Coffeemaker
❏ Microwave
❏ Refrigerator
❏ Table and four utility chairs
❏ Cups, plates, and bowls
❏ Knives, forks, spoons, and carving knife
❏ Basic tool box with pliers, a screw driver, and a hammer
❏ Water dispenser
❏ Cabinets to lock valuables
❏ Live plants

CONFERENCE ROOM

Conference rooms are generally utilitarian, but this is another opportunity to use decorators to determine the best color combinations, as well as the style and size of the table and chairs. Depositions, attorney/client conferences, and other stressful activities are conducted in the conference room. It is important to furnish the conference rooms to minimize stress on everybody involved, especially yourself. Art work and plants are excellent ways to make the conference room a more pleasant place. You may want to provide a bare white wall or a projection screen for presentations, and a monitor for viewing videotapes. A dimmer switch in the conference room is very helpful during PowerPoint, video, and other presentations.

Conference rooms are often effectively combined with a firm's law library. In order to avoid interruptions by people coming in to look for books, a protocol should be prearranged for library users. It is very easy for a library to become rather messy, with pocket parts, supplements, and other paperbound volumes scattered about. The room should be kept as neat as possible to support your image as a well-run law firm.

FILING SYSTEMS

One of the areas that should not be neglected in setting up an office is a filing system. Many office supply houses will help you devise a system that works in your space. The law office management sections of the bar associations also provide help in determining what kind of filing system you should have and the relative costs of each one. The filing system that you choose at the outset can follow you throughout your practice, so you should start with a system that can be expanded in the future in almost an unlimited fashion.

MAINTAINING THE OFFICE

Once you have set up your office, you need to make sure that it is maintained consistently. A regular cleaning service should be supplemented with additional care, such as carpet cleaning and window washing. Someone on your staff should watch for worn or stained carpet, upholstery, and wall coverings, which can communicate the wrong message in even the most successful law firm. Do not forget to periodically purge files, as the large amount of paperwork generated by a law office can be unwieldy. This is something that you should provide for in your office procedures.

chapter six:
Equipment and Furniture

Any business needs some basic furnishings and equipment to be able to operate. The initial expenses for such things can be quite considerable. Your choices in these items can range from the simple to the extravagant. For the new office, it often makes a lot of sense to explore all options available for acquiring these items. A listing of the basic components needed as you set up your office is on page 56. A listing of some advice for office supplies is on page 57.

TO BUY, LEASE, OR RENT

The furniture for the reception area, lawyers' offices, and staff spaces can be purchased, leased, or rented. Some companies will lease furniture for a year or longer, while rentals are usually for less than a year. The decision whether to buy, lease, or rent furniture and equipment will depend upon the finances of the practice and the availability of discounts from vendors. The cost of furnishings and equipment can affect your balance sheet, and should be discussed with your CPA or other tax advisor as you determine the capital outlay that you will be required to make in beginning your law practice. You would not want your leather sofa to affect your cash flow or your ability to borrow working capital.

Leasing equipment is often a good way of obtaining the latest, state-of-the-art equipment. When improved equipment becomes available, the lease can be renegotiated and the equipment can be upgraded. If the equipment is purchased, your only option is to sell it or trade it in for new equipment. Purchasing equipment requires capital, whereas leasing may only depend upon your credit rating.

Large office equipment, such as photocopiers, can be obtained from used equipment dealers. This is an area where a consultant can be extremely valuable. When law firms close down or upgrade their equipment, many used items can be made available. Sometimes all you have to do is take over the payments of a leased piece of equipment.

An extensive market in reconditioned copiers provides a large cost savings opportunity for lawyers. A new copy machine, which may obligate the lawyer or office to a $30,000 lease, may be obtained second-hand with warranty for as little as $7,000–$10,000, or leased at a comparable monthly expense. The cost of paper, toner, and machine maintenance can be substantial, so any copy machine should have a document-counting device, preferably with software that allows for recording the number of copies made and charging it to the file for which the document is created.

New office furniture is always an option. Furniture stores often give favorable credit terms. As your practice expands, the furniture dealer is useful in obtaining additional pieces within the price range and style consistent with what is already established.

Finding Less Expensive Furniture

Office furniture can also be obtained through used furniture dealers or auction houses. The latter may provide opportunities for obtaining fine furniture—even antiques—at very reasonable prices. The entire office may not be furnished all at once, but important pieces of furniture can be obtained over a period of time.

One of the most important pieces—and something that should not be skimped on—is office chairs. Chairs for lawyers and staff may be your single most important acquisition as you furnish your office. Seating should provide excellent support and positioning suitable for the work being done over the course of many hours each day. The chair's size, structure, firmness, upholstery, arm height and width, and adjustability should all be taken into consideration. Never purchase a chair until you have sat in it, preferably at a desk set up similarly to the one where it will be used.

Assuming the lease of a law office that has closed down or is moving can provide opportunities for a beginning law firm. Many firms close their doors and leave their furniture and equipment behind. Here again, the law office management section of bar associations can be helpful with this kind of networking. Law book salespeople or law office resource material sales representatives can also be helpful, because they have access to many law firms and can tell you which ones are downsizing, expanding, or actually shutting down, and where libraries and furniture are for sale.

Newspaper classified ads can be a good source of information regarding furniture—not just for the furniture itself, but for dealers who may have a wide selection of office furniture, new or used, that will save you time shopping for your selections. The Internet may also be a good source for information, local and otherwise, with regard to office furniture.

With each significant acquisition, either personal or for the firm, you should carefully compare the cost of purchasing with the cost of leasing. The lease is likely to be higher in total payout, because it will include interest, taxes, and other charges that the leasing company has to pay. Purchased equipment may seem less expensive, but the cost of property taxes and interest on borrowed money should be factored into the calculations.

Basic Office Equipment Checklist

❏ Small copy machine
❏ Scanner
❏ Portable tape recorders
❏ Word processor
❏ Dictating unit
❏ Transcription unit
❏ Fast black and white laser printer
❏ Fireproof safe for wills, important documents, and accounts receivable records
❏ Postage meter
❏ Paper cutter
❏ Staplers and staple removers
❏ Filing cabinets
❏ Check protector

Office Supplies Checklist

NOTE: *Discuss office needs with an experienced legal secretary.*

❏ Stationery
❏ Pens and pencils
❏ Felt-tipped markers
❏ Envelopes, including manila
❏ Two-hole punch
❏ Three-hole punch
❏ Telephone message books
❏ Rubber stamps
❏ Ink pads
❏ Legal pads
❏ Paper clips, stapler, and staples
❏ Scissors
❏ Files
❏ Checkbooks
❏ Address labels (firm name)
❏ Toner for printers and copiers

TELEPHONES

Beyond the furnishings, the most important office tool may be the telephone system. As stated in the discussion on business formation fundamentals, the telephone system is one of the key components of any business, and telephone companies provide many features for you.

You should have a minimum of three telephone lines and two telephone numbers. One of the lines should be dedicated for your fax, and a number should be dedicated to that line as well. At the very least, one of the lines should be for yourself and one for your staff. As far as peripherals attached to your phone system, you should have at the very minimum caller ID, speakerphone, mute, hands-free, hold, do not disturb, and conferencing features. You should also consider using a DSL line so you can access simultaneous data and voice. This is discussed in the section called "Computer Hardware." (see page 62.)

The use of cell phones is now critical for business purposes, and this will necessitate the acquisition of another telephone number. There may be a possibility of having the cell phone number connected to your office system. You should check with your telephone company to see if this can be arranged.

Generally speaking, it is more practical to buy your telephone sets and fax machines rather than lease them. However, if your system has multiple components that are going to be upgraded and improved over the years, you may want to discuss leasing those systems with your provider. You may then be in a better position to negotiate future leases to include the improvements as they occur. This is a practical way of extending your lease to include later improvements from which you can benefit.

To help make your phone system a useful tool, develop a *Telephone Intake Form* like the one on page 59. This will often be the first piece of information to go into your file and will ensure that vital, but easily overlooked, information is obtained.

Telephone Intake Form

Date and time of call: _____

Caller's full name: _____

Telephone numbers, including fax: _____

_____

Brief description of the problem: _____

_____

Caller's home address, street in addition to P.O. Box: _____

_____

_____

Appointment date and time: _____

Criminal case: _____

    Jail or court: _____

    Amount of bail: _____

    Witnesses for the interview: _____

Maps, diagrams, and photos for interview: _____

_____

Physical evidence for interview: _____

Retainer or fee: _____

Personal injury case: _____

    Date of the injury: _____

    Place where injury occurred: _____

    Injuries: _____

    Witnesses: _____

Send letter confirming appointment and set diary date: _____

NOTE: *When a client meets with you, use the **Client Interview Form** (page 131) to complete the basis for engagement.*

COMPUTERS

Whether you are a tech-savvy lawyer or one who would vastly prefer quill and parchment, your new law practice will require a diverse array of hardware and software. Choosing the computers for yourself and your staff may be the single most important technical decision that you are going to have to make. Do not attempt it alone, and do not rely on the salesperson in your local computer store to advise you. Seek the expertise of a computer consultant who has both deep technical knowledge and particular experience in the needs of law firms. Ask your professional colleagues or your local bar association for recommendations, and interview the consultant before commencing, just as you would any potential employee. Be cautious of consultants whose solutions are based upon equipment that you must purchase from them.

This book cannot offer exhaustive details on computer systems, but it can provide some guidelines that will assist you in making your decisions. In general, you should look for a number of qualities in your computer system, including speed, memory, expandability, flexibility, compatibility, networking, security, and backup. You want to build a system that reflects the way you actually work and is easily adaptable as your practice grows. While hardware and software are quickly obsolete, look for solid, proven systems that can be upgraded as necessary.

You may have a computer that you have used throughout college and law school, and you may feel comfortable with that particular system. Ask your consultant whether it is practical to open up your law office with that equipment. Discuss your preferences, the relative merits and compatibility of PCs and Macs for law professionals, and the essential hardware and software for your business.

Computer choices are personal, but they are also driven by the nature of your practice. Keep in mind that the lawyers and staff using the equipment may have a wide range of technical expertise, and the system should accommodate everyone comfortably. It should allow your *techie* law clerks and legal secretaries to speed through documents using all available shortcuts, and also should be user-friendly for the lawyer who types using the hunt-and-peck method.

While it may be tempting to equip your office for the staff you envision acquiring over the next year, it makes more sense to start small and expand gradually. Set up your office for the lawyers and staff you have now and anticipate hiring in the next quarter. Test that equipment and make sure it meets your needs. Then, as you increase the size of your staff, add components, providing the fastest new equipment to the most skilled users—usually, your legal secretaries.

As you are planning your computer system, consider carefully the way you actually work. For example, do you perform a lot of your work on a laptop? Do you send and receive email and keep important information in a handheld device, such as a Palm Pilot or BlackBerry? Do you prefer to dictate rather than type? Do you handwrite drafts on paper or on an electronic tablet? Do you use speech recognition software? Do you use videoconferencing? Do you use e-discovery? The computer world is full of dazzling gadgets—make sure the ones you purchase are practical and useful for your business.

Computer Hardware

Depending on the size of your practice, your system will include a number of servers, computers, monitors, printers, scanners, projectors, backup power supplies, and other external components, such as handheld devices, mice, backup drives, and so on. It is not necessary to spend huge sums of money to buy effective computer hardware. High-performance systems become less and less expensive as newer models appear on the scene.

Long-term usefulness is critical. It is better to spend a little more on a solid, mainstream system than to look for the lowest-priced model and risk losing data when it crashes. In general, avoid used equipment, which is often under-powered and not easily upgraded. An efficient new system that has adequate capacity for your needs can be purchased for a reasonable cost, and more importantly, will be covered by warranty.

Your office system should accommodate both desktop and laptop computers. With more and more lawyers drafting their own documents on laptops, docking stations with extra monitors and full-size keyboards are far more efficient than desktop models. At the same time, your secretarial and accounting staff will find desktop systems more practical.

Look for speed, power, and memory capacity as you are building your system. Get a computer with the fastest processor, clock rate (expressed in *gigahertz* (GHz)), Random Access Memory (RAM) (expressed in *megabytes* (MB)), and hard disk capacity (expressed in *gigabytes* (GB)). Consider which elements will allow you the most power and flexibility as your practice grows—and understand that as soon as you have purchased your system, a faster one will come onto the market. Your consultant should be able to advise you on the best operating system for your needs.

Purchase the largest monitors you can afford, and nothing smaller than seventeen-inch screens. While flat-screen monitors are still more expensive, they free up valuable desktop space, and are both practical and handsome.

Your system should have built-in connectivity—Ethernet or wireless—to allow Internet access, email, and other forms of networking, and you may want a modem as backup. Even a small office must have a networked computer system that allows the attorneys, secretaries, and paralegals to share files. Otherwise, a great deal of nonproductive time is spent retrieving documents created at one workstation for use at another.

Your system should also come equipped with a powerful firewall for security, often as part of the operating system. Be sure your office computer person regularly installs the necessary *patches* to keep the system current. CD/DVD burners are very practical, as are USB ports on the front of the computer, which allow for a variety of things to be plugged into the computer on an as-needed basis.

Document scanners enable paper documents to be scanned into the office network. *Optical character reading* (OCR) software associated with scanners translates scanned documents into text files. Scanners reduce the need for storage space as files are closed, though you must balance the cost of paper storage and retrieval against the cost of scanning. Whether you store old files in electronic or paper form, an efficient and easily understood indexing system should be established to make sure that files can be retrieved if they are needed.

Because law offices can become dependent upon computer systems for everything from creating documents to billing to carrying out legal research, a significant system failure can be very costly and disruptive. A backup power source, known as an *uninterrupted power supply* (UPS), is essential to protect the system from power failures.

A data backup system that automatically copies and stores files is also critical to file security. You should establish a backup protocol, including how frequently backups are made, where and how they are stored, and how long they are kept before erasing and re-recording. Your backup system is only useful if it is consistently maintained and monitored.

If you are opening a trial practice or anticipate making presentations, consider adding a digital projector to your system. Compact projectors can be connected to a laptop computer and used with PowerPoint to display documents and photographs to juries and other audiences. Video projectors permit documents to be displayed on a screen without having been scanned and stored into the computer. Both systems work with a portable screen and are frequently used in trials and motion hearings. Be sure to stock spare bulbs and instruct projector users in proper system use and replacement of bulbs.

Communications Checklist

❏ Obtain telephone and fax numbers, as well as email addresses. Get lines dedicated to these numbers and obtain a domain name for a website.

❏ Secure a dedicated line for your computer.

❏ Acquire cell phones and make certain that the numbers are portable from vendor to vendor.

❏ Obtain the highest-speed Internet service available within your budget.

❏ Engage a printer for initial stationery, cards, announcements, and other printed material. Although you may print these things on a computer, you will want some high quality stock for special needs.

❏ Make certain that you utilize phone services as much as your budget allows—call forwarding, call waiting, speakerphone, remote access to call forwarding, teleconferencing, caller ID.

Computer Software

Your computer's software allows you and your staff to carry out the scores of necessary tasks that comprise your business, such as the drafting of text documents, calendaring, database management, accounting, billing, document and case management, and many other tasks.

As with the purchase of hardware, it is wise to acquire the latest software that your budget will allow. Stick with mainstream programs and update them regularly. It is not in your best interest to be one of the first users of a new software program. You want to spend your time working efficiently rather than trying to solve the vendor's problems. Most critically, make sure that the programs you select are compatible with each other to streamline operations and eliminate the duplication of work.

Software programs constitute the heart of your law practice, and there are certain ones that you should have when you start. Some are necessary, and others are desirable. The following are the five types of programs that you must have to begin your practice.

1. Word processing software—which is used to prepare correspondence, contracts, and other documents—is the most important place to begin. The standard cutting, pasting, copying, and other editing features of word processing programs are supplemented by the ability to number pages, paragraphs, and to prepare tables of contents. You can also combine graphics with text and create stationery and labels.

2. Time and billing software is essential to a law firm, and your system should be initiated at the beginning with the capability of expanding and improving as your firm grows. It not only can track the time, but produce bills and other financial information, such as costs on a specific matter. Programs that accommodate UBTMS codes, created through the efforts of the ABA, are also used by many insurance companies and other businesses. These codes use activity and task descriptions that permit coding the particular phase, the course of litigation, and the specific task being carried out, as well as the time expended for which a bill will be presented. As clients increasingly expect a detailed description of work that has been carried out, billing software becomes an essential tool.

3. Accounting software ties in directly with your billing and accounting systems, giving you access to the general ledger, accounts payable, and your current cash balances both in your own accounts and in your trust accounts. It can also tell you what your accounts receivable and accounts payable look like. Your accountant can access your financial information easily so you do not have to provide this information at the last minute for the preparation of your tax returns.

4. Virus protection software is critical, and must be updated often because the viruses are constantly being created and threaten the heart of your office systems. Software finds and removes viruses that might get into your system and can be programmed to check each entry that you put into your computer, survey the hard drive of your computer routinely, and monitor email messages to determine if they contain a virus. Newer anti-virus software also contains anti-spam, anti-spyware, and anti-adware software programs, which are essential to your system's security.

5. Tape backup software comes with the tape backup unit that is installed in your computer. It is the most reliable way to back up your entire computer system, but it is only as reliable as the staff responsible for its operation—it will not change tapes for you. The backup system must be monitored routinely, with someone on your staff having that responsibility. Backup files store your databases in case of natural disasters, such as hurricanes, floods, and earthquakes, as well as fires and thefts. One certain way to hamper the operation of a law practice is for important components to be stolen or destroyed with no backup available.

These five types of software are the basics for beginning your practice. The following types of software are important, and should be acquired as soon as your finances permit.

- Document management software allows you to find documents created during a specific time period, containing specific words, or created by a particular person in your firm for a certain client or matter. The documents are catalogued and easily retrievable. Web-based document management systems now allow multi-lawyer collaboration, analysis, and secure storage of vast amounts of documentation.

- Case management software is designed to keep track of specific contacts, case files, certain events, and diary information. It can be designed for detailed file management, especially in a litigation practice.

- Spreadsheet software programs are specifically designed for financial applications, which can include financial projections, tax calculations, and other related documentation. Discuss this with your accountant beforehand. Spreadsheet software should have the flexibility to grow with the development of your firm.

- Communications and remote-access software connects one computer to other computers for email and research on electronic libraries, such as Lexis and Westlaw. It also allows you to communicate with your office from your computer at home or elsewhere while you are traveling.

- Document assembly software works with your word processing software, case management software, and document management software to aid the creation of documents by providing information about the client or case for which the document is being produced. Document assembly is expanded upon in the next section.

- Conflict of interest software is very important to a growing firm, as it determines if there is a conflict of interest in a new matter. This software works with the time and billing, case management, and document management software programs. This is another example of the integration of the various software programs in your system.
- Special software programs are constantly being created for specific applications. An example is a practice-specific application for probate, family law, criminal law, and other areas of the law. Programs are specifically created for tax preparation and calculation. Collaborative discovery applications and e-discovery are rapidly gaining popularity.
- Presentation software is used by lawyers to provide graphic presentations to clients in transactional practice, or provide demonstrative evidence in a trial or arbitration setting. A PowerPoint presentation can be very effective. The relative importance of certain aspects of the client's case can be shown graphically with pie charts, graphs, text, and the use of color.
- Litigation support software enables the litigator to examine the texts of depositions, search them, and annotate them. It also allows the cataloguing of documents that are obtained from discovery. Trial preparation is aided immensely by the ability to coordinate specific areas of deposition testimony and document the portions retrieved by searches on

their contents. Coordinating the litigation support software with the presentation software for trial preparation is very helpful.

The software programs discussed support many of the functions that you will find necessary in starting your practice. Some of them overlap, and you should consult with your computer or technology consultant to determine which current software programs are best for your practice. For example, litigation support software may have many of the features of case or practice management software that you need for a litigation practice, and you may not need to purchase separate software programs. A document-assembly program may also contain many related functions, eliminating the need for some other software.

Most personal computers will include software to perform the basic tasks necessary in a law office, with the exception of a billing program. While Microsoft Word is currently the most commonly used word processing program and will be more easily retrieved by clients to whom emailed attachments are sent, Word Perfect has traditionally been more popular in the law office environment. Regardless of the choice of word processing program, there will be some documents, such as spreadsheets and charts, that cannot readily be created or transmitted in a program intended primarily for word processing. Therefore, a useful software addition is Adobe Acrobat, which allows the conversion of files into readable *Portable Document Format* (PDF) files.

The office computer system must have sufficient capacity to operate email, which is of increasing importance. Many courts, such as some federal courts in California, have gone to a fully electronic system, which encourages email filings. Internet access, with a fast, reliable connection, is a necessity. A computerized office calendar program should be obtained. Such programs are available within standard word processing programs as well as in stand-alone programs. A useful software accessory is a media player that supports the digital projection of photographs and tapes previously stored on video.

There are law office management software programs on the market. Find the one that is most suitable for you by talking with other attorneys and computer consultants, as well as law office management sections of the *American Bar Association* (ABA), state bar associations, and local bar associations.

Generally speaking, software products should be evaluated for upgrading approximately every two to three years. Exceptions to this are virus protection programs, which need to be monitored and upgraded every few weeks. Also, practice-specific programs should be upgraded semiannually. The backup system may last for five or six years without upgrading, unless there are programs that require modifications of your backup system. The upgrading should take place on a case-by-case basis.

Document Assembly

The use of forms is pervasive in businesses. Documents that contain boilerplate elements (such as letters, contracts, and pleadings) each have a set of repetitive formalities that can be made into templates, so they can be quickly available when needed. The computer has elevated the use of forms to a higher dimension, and enables a user to take advantage of the computer's capacity to store information in a database by merging that information into documents. It can draw the elements together and assemble them into a single document, while interacting with users and making decisions based on information taken from the database or from the users.

A document-assembly system contains three basic elements. The first is a database or data source, which contains information organized in areas (called *fields*) with an identifying name. The second is the templates, which are documents or partial documents containing field names that provide links to the fields in the data source. The third component is the document-assembly engine, which is a program that merges the data from the database or data source into the templates. It may be a word processing program or software designed for a particular document assembly.

The system begins by the creation of a record in the database. The computer presents a series of questions to you in order to obtain the information needed for that database. The information is stored and is ready to be used to produce a variety of documents.

When you need to assemble a document, the computer prompts you to identify the document you want, and it then merges the information from the database into the desired document. During that process, the computer determines the appropriate information from the database and incorporates it. Information that is necessary but is not in the database is requested. Document-assembly templates give you a way of storing precedents and keeping them in a reliable and accessible form. The documents that are produced are much better-looking than an old-fashioned form, and beyond these aesthetics, the practitioner can produce documents that have the same apparent quality as those produced by large firms. This gives the practitioner who is starting out the advantage of a more level playing field with competitors.

There are essentially three types of document-assembly programs. The first is programs for distinct areas of the practice, such as family law, probate, or bankruptcy. These are useful because you get the precedents of the program developers. They have the least flexibility in your ability to modify the database and templates. The second type is made up of the programs that commit you to create your own templates and database. Such programs are flexible, and you can individualize your own templates and databases. However, these programs require you to learn new program commands. The third type is word processing programs and database programs. They give you the most flexibility, because you create your own database and templates. However, you must also assume more responsibility, dealing with the more complex programming of functions involved in word processing programs.

Talk with your computer consultant to determine which of these types of programs are best for your practice, particularly as you are starting your business. Your decision will also depend upon your knowledge and expertise in using the various programs and hardware. Your technical advisor will help you develop a plan for managing your document-assembly needs. Most importantly, you should devote specific times to develop the databases and templates for your system. The contributions of your staff can be invaluable, along with the consultations of your expert.

As with many aspects of using computers, you will find that you spend more time than you have allotted in the creation of databases and designing templates. Consequently, planning those time periods is important and providing limitations as to the use of time is necessary. Start with the simplest documents and graduate to the more complex ones as they become necessary, and as you and your staff develop skills to prepare them.

Part of your plan should include a routine review of the data used in the templates and from the database to make them more generic and efficient. This review should be made with an eye toward the use of positive and pleasing language as shown in the correspondence examples in this book. The proofreading of documents is made much easier because you can develop a proof sheet template that will print out the information from the database. It will be easier to modify or correct it when used in other templates.

Document assembly provides speed, reliability, accuracy, and cost-effectiveness in document production. It is especially important for practitioners starting out, when their resources may not be as extensive as larger firms and they may not have the support staff of those firms. It is a way for beginning practitioners to present correspondence or court documents that look professional and have the characteristics of the highest quality of documentation.

Day-to-Day Operations

Your computer consultant will be able to advise you on the setup of your system, but you will also need day-to-day support for a variety of technical issues that arise. While an attorney or staff person can assist with minor computer-related problems, a computer technician who can respond on very short notice should also be available to resolve infrequent, but potentially vexing computer failures that will arise. In smaller law firms, a contract maintenance service should be engaged. As with any service business, references should be obtained before allowing a technician to repair a computer system for you or to make significant alterations.

Your computer consultant or your technician will also be able to advise you on the necessary hardware and software upgrades to keep your system current. It is his or her job to keep up with the marketplace, and you should take advantage of his or her expertise.

Along with establishing other computer and office protocols, you will need to establish a training protocol for lawyers and staff personnel to assure that expensive hardware and software are used properly. A skilled staff person, an outside consultant, or a training school can handle this task.

In certain specialties, such as family law, criminal law, and tax law, it is common to find lawyers' study groups that meet periodically to go over the latest legislation or court decisions in their area. This is also a good opportunity to compare notes with respect to technical experts, technology that is suitable for your specialty, and law office procedures in general. If you cannot find a study group in your area of the law, it is to your advantage to start one. Additionally, the bar association law office management sections are invaluable in helping you choose a computer system for your office.

Computer Planning Checklist

❑ PC vs. Mac
❑ Desktop and laptop integration
❑ Docking stations
❑ Essential system components—processor, clock rate, RAM, hard disk
❑ Monitors
❑ Scanners
❑ Projectors
❑ Handheld devices
❑ Backup power source
❑ Firewall
❑ CD/DVD burner
❑ USB ports
❑ Word processing software
❑ Time and billing software
❑ Calendaring software
❑ Accounting software
❑ Virus protection software, including anti-spam, anti-spyware, and anti-adware
❑ Tape backup software or other data backup system
❑ Document management software
❑ Case management software
❑ Spreadsheet software
❑ Practice-specific software
❑ Presentation software
❑ Litigation support software
❑ Media player
❑ Adobe Acrobat
❑ Law office management software
❑ Document-assembly systems
❑ Computer training
❑ Computer maintenance and technical support
❑ Upgrading

chapter seven:
Personnel

One of the most important factors that a beginning law firm must keep in mind at all times is that client communication is paramount. If the client gets the notion that you are indifferent or unable or unwilling to communicate, the client will go elsewhere for an attentive professional. For this reason, it is important to have someone in the office to deal with clients personally, whether clients come into the office, call on the phone, or communicate by email.

Client communications is only one of the many tasks that needs to be accomplished in order to keep your practice running. Having chosen your office space, you may now want to decide how the clerical, secretarial, and administrative work is going to be done for your practice.

However, before even thinking about hiring your first employee, you must keep in mind that all personnel are entitled to certain legal rights, and you should know what those legal rights are. Attorneys have historically been some of the worst offenders when it comes to employment-related laws, and you do not want your new business being one of those offenders. Generally, a sense of fairness and sensitivity will help you avoid personnel problems. Nevertheless, there are certain legal responsibilities that an employer must observe, and you should be aware of them when you start your practice. Some of the main legal requirements you should be aware of fall into the following two main categories.

    1. Civil Rights

- *Civil Rights Act of 1964.* This act makes it unlawful for employers with fifteen or more employees to discriminate against people based on race, color, religion, national origin, or sex with regard to hiring and employment.

- *Age Discrimination and Employment Act of 1967.* This act prohibits firms with twenty or more employees from discriminating against workers 40 years of age or over.

- *Pregnancy Discrimination Act of 1978.* This act requires that pregnancy be treated as any other medical condition.

- *Rehabilitation Act of 1973.* This act prohibits discrimination against physically or mentally handicapped people in federal contracts.

- *Immigration, Reform and Control Act of 1986.* Employers must verify proof of citizenship and legal residency of their employees in the United States. Each employer must keep a completed federal I-9 form for each employee hired after 1986. This is a very important business requirement.

- *Americans with Disabilities Act of 1990.* This act prohibits employers of fifteen or more employees from discriminating against handicapped people, and requires providing them with accommodations that do not pose an undue hardship.

- *Older Workers Benefit Protection Act of 1990.* This prohibits discrimination with respect to employee benefits based on age and regulates early retirement benefits.

2. Work Safety and Fairness

- *Occupational Safety and Health Act of 1970 (OSHA).* Employers must provide safe working conditions for workers. In addition to this requirement is the *Hazard Communication Standard,* which is a means of informing employees about hazards and how to respond to them.

- *Employee Polygraph Protection Act of 1988.* This act makes it unlawful for employers to request lie detector tests from employees or job applicants.

- Workers' Compensation Laws. These are laws on the books of the various states, and the requirements and benefits are variable. You should check your state laws with the help of your insurance broker and your accountant.

- *Employee Retirement Income Security Act of 1974 (ERISA).* This act governs operations of pensions and retirement benefits provided by private employers. If you have joined a retirement trust plan for employees, this may affect you. The employee trust program is a way for small enterprises to give employees benefits by joining a larger group. Check with your insurance broker to see if any of these requirements apply to you.

- Posting notices in a prominent location. This usually is done in the employee lounge area so that there is no doubt that the employees have an opportunity to see all of the required postings. Check with your insurance broker and your accountant to determine which ones are required to be posted.

LAW FIRM PERSONNEL

Law firm personnel generally fall into three categories—line personnel, line support personnel, and staff personnel. *Line personnel* are those people who directly earn money for the enterprise. The line personnel are lawyers whose billing and retainers provide the income of the enterprise. Law clerks and paralegals are included in this category, because they too generate actual income for the firm. Sometimes, the profit margin in the billable time of paralegals and law clerks is higher than that of the lawyers themselves. *Line support personnel* are those people who work closely with the line personnel, enabling them to generate income by performing the functions of legal assistants and other technical aspects of supporting the line personnel.

Staff personnel are those individuals whose work does not directly generate income, but benefits the firm as a whole. Receptionists, bookkeepers, accountants, office administrators, office managers, and human resource directors fall into this category. In some cases, some of the more technical support staff may be outside specialists who perform those functions for the firm more economically, such as accountants, bookkeepers, graphic artists, or human resource directors.

The requirements for the various categories of personnel are distinctly different from each other. The interviewing and hiring of the categories of personnel is particularly important, and the personality types of people for each category should be carefully examined. For example, a polished trial lawyer who is an extrovert serves a completely different function from a bookkeeper who may enjoy working quietly and may be perfectly content to produce prodigious work in near solitude. Knowing the different personality types that are required for different personnel functions is a very important aspect of establishing the makeup of the firm from the beginning.

The sources of the various categories of personnel may differ from each other as well. Line support personnel, such as legal assistants, may be obtained from employment agencies or through legal newspaper advertisements. The same may hold true for staff positions, such as bookkeepers, office administrators, and similar functions.

Lawyers quite often come to the firm through personal contact, referral, or by invitation from the lawyers already in the firm. Oftentimes, lawyers may be obtained through legal newspaper advertisements as well, particularly when the firm is looking for a specific type of legal experience. The use of professional placement services or *headhunters* may not be cost-effective in the beginning of your firm, but it is worthwhile for you to inquire of their cost.

Paralegals may be obtained through advertisements or by referral, but quite often they are former legal assistants who have advanced themselves to the paralegal position through experience working for law firms and for lawyers. Law clerks, on the other hand, most frequently come from law schools, often as summer interns, or work part-time and attend law school at the same time.

Your local newspapers and other periodicals will have advertisements for these and other legal temp services, and many times individual classified ads will be helpful as well. You can make use of this resource not only for staff, but also for law library materials, civic organizations, and other materials and services that you will need to begin your law practice.

In general, you want to look for the basic things in all of the people you hire as staff, assistants, paralegals, law clerks, and associates. You want to make sure they have good references, good work habits, and skills appropriate to their titles. In large metropolitan areas, temporary employment agencies can provide all of these services for you.

Employment agencies are available in most locations and can help with the hiring process. However, if you employ someone through an employment agency, this may add a great deal of expense to your staff costs. The employment agency is entitled to a fee from you if you hire the person they recommend.

ADDITIONAL ASSISTANCE

Contracting functions outside the firm can be helpful to a law firm that is starting out. If the lawyers become so busy that court appearances and other calendar items conflict, contract lawyers can be brought in to handle the simpler, more routine matters and give the lawyers in the firm more freedom to focus on the most important calendar items. Paralegals can be brought in by contract as well, because there are professional groups of paralegals whose business is contracting themselves out for specific projects for law firms.

With regard to outside contract services, one of the most rewarding ways to obtain seasoned personnel is through organizations that specialize in the employment of people who have retired or who are over age 40. This is a way for people with considerable and valuable experience to add value to your law firm, because they can save you time and give you practical advice. This is especially true in certain specialties, such as probate, estate and trust, insurance defense, plaintiff's personal injury, drunk driving, real estate, and other law specialties that have their own *culture* in their respective areas.

Specialized staff positions, such as human resources, directors, bookkeepers, and technical graphics experts, can also be contracted. The resources that are obtained by contract expand the capacity of the line personnel at a time when the resources of the firm may not support such people full time. This is also a very good way to fill in the gaps of a beginning law firm, allowing it to grow and expand without having to cope with raising the capital to afford such resources right away.

If the partnership or group of lawyers exceeds three or four, it is advisable to hire an *office administrator*. This person is typically a very experienced legal secretary who has experience in law office administration, particularly in the firm's specialty. A firm of ten to fifteen lawyers will have a need for professional, outside consulting for some management issues. A law firm of fifteen or more lawyers must have highly trained law office management. Human resources

issues are now so complex and involved with statutory regulations that small firms often turn them over to outside
consultants, while large firms are more likely to manage
human resources issues internally.

When a firm is in its beginning phase and there are only
one or two lawyers, basic functions such as typing correspondence, briefs, billings, and other typing needs can be
done by an outside clerical or typing service. You may also
decide to use a secretarial service, where a secretary can
come to your office a few days a week and do the filing,
typing, and other office functions that are necessary. These
are two types of contract workers for whom you do not
have to set up the usual withholding accounts, as you do
with regular employees.

Such options give the beginning law firm a lot of flexibility
and means of expanding its impact without having the burden of maintaining full-time personnel when capital is limited. Additionally, you only use them when you need them,
and you avoid a lot of dead time for your employees when
the workload is erratic, as it may be when you are starting
out in your law practice, regardless of how many lawyers
are with you.

If you have a high quality secretarial or typing service doing
the necessary pleadings and other things that you need, you
may want to have someone in the office to take care of
answering the telephone, filing, and other relatively low-skilled
tasks. These people can be local college or law school students
who can be available for you on certain days of the week. It
is even possible to have two or three of them working for you
part-time. For example, one student works in the morning and

one in the afternoon, so that you have full-time coverage of your telephones and filing.

If you are sharing office space, you may want to make an arrangement with others in that situation to use the talents of secretaries and other administrative staff, and share their expenses.

WHO TO HIRE

Before selecting any staff, it is a necessary and practical exercise to go over in your mind the kinds of people that you want to hire. Naturally, everyone wants pleasant, cooperative, and happy people around when running a law office. Rarely can you tell from an interview whether people are going to fulfill these expectations. Their résumés and work history, including references, can give you a good idea as to the quality of their work. You should talk to those personal reference contacts as a way to determine their work habits and behavior in the office relating to others, especially clients.

When beginning your law firm, two functions are crucial and are best performed by two different people. The first is the bookkeeping function. An accountant familiar with the practice of law firms should be obtained immediately. The accountant can either perform the bookkeeping function for you in that office or can recommend a bookkeeper to you. It can be helpful when the bookkeeper and the accountant have worked together in the past and know how to work efficiently with each other.

It is important to find a bookkeeper who will give you continuity over a long period of time, because you will need bookkeeping and accounting information for taxes and other business-reporting purposes. You want someone in that position who loves to do detailed work. Very few extroverts truly enjoy doing detailed work. If you only have one staff person to be assistant, receptionist, and bookkeeper, you may want to outsource the bookkeeping function until you can afford to hire an in-house bookkeeper.

The second necessary person is a legal assistant or secretary. Quite often, the first full-time employee that you will hire is an assistant or a secretary. Occasionally, the secretary will do double duty as a receptionist, and you want to look for the gregarious, outgoing type of person who will give your firm a pleasant image in the minds of others.

In beginning your law practice, it is probably wise to have, if possible, an experienced legal secretary or a legal assistant from the start. Not only can they do more work because they are experienced, but they can also give you good advice. As you progress and acquire more staff, such as paralegals and associates, you can increase the secretarial capacity for your firm by bringing in accomplished assistants who can learn how to become legal assistants from experienced staff and may be less expensive for you at the outset.

THE INTERVIEW

Nothing substitutes for the personal interview. You want to hire someone who is pleasant, articulate, dresses neatly, and shows signs of having good personal habits—which can relate directly to work habits. You should require at least three references from past employers. Other types of personal references, such as friends, ministers, and teachers, are fine, but employment references are essential and must be followed up. You can learn a great deal about the person you interviewed during a pleasant conversation with someone who is giving a reference. If the candidate has limited employment experience, you should get a personal reference from each prior employer.

When you call to discuss the applicant, you should keep your manner as pleasant and positive as possible in order to obtain information without having to go into cross-examination. If the prior employment experience was pleasant, you will probably get a happy narration of positive things. If the employment situation was not positive, you will probably have difficulty getting any information of a positive kind, or possibly of any kind from a prior employer. Consider this carefully before you hire someone who had a bad experience with a prior employer. Such bad experiences happen all the time and no one can be faulted for having them. Nevertheless, if a person has a pattern of *personality differences* with employers, you should consider that a red flag and be cautious.

Since the legal secretary or assistant is going to be doing the bulk of the clerical work on your behalf, you should have some idea of the proficiency of the applicant. This can be determined by standard tests that are given in secretarial schools, so that you know how many words per minute the applicant can type, as well as what software and computer systems the applicant has proficiency in.

A person who is realistic in personal expectations when applying for such a job as a legal assistant should make their technical proficiency available to you without any trouble. Anyone who is reluctant for you to learn how proficient their error-free typing is should be given a very low consideration for hiring.

THE LEGAL ASSISTANT

The term *legal assistant* has various connotations in the many jurisdictions in this country. In some areas, it is a term of art, meaning someone who is equal to a paralegal and governed roughly by regulation or by statute. In other areas, it is an interchangeable term for legal secretary. The term *paralegal* is generally defined as someone who works under the direct supervision of a lawyer, and who does legal research, memo drafting, pleadings drafting, and other things preliminary to the work the lawyer does.

The use of paralegals is something that can be beneficial to a beginning law firm. In fact, there are contract paralegals who can do a great deal of work for you, which you can bill to your clients. Such billings can become a significant *profit center* for you, as well as making you look very efficient because you can handle more than one matter at a time.

Legal research and pleadings drafting can be two of the most important areas for the use of paralegals. In a practice that is geared toward transactional activities, paralegals can be even more important. They can write a rough draft of some contracts, trusts, wills, agreements, and the other tedious and time-consuming documents that can then be reviewed by the practicing lawyer.

In looking for a paralegal, you should make certain that they give you at least three references, preferably from employers. The use of work samples can be important, as long as you can assure yourself that the interviewee actually drafted the material that is shown as an exemplar.

On many occasions, *law clerks*, generally defined as law students working in law offices during vacation time or part-time during weekdays, can do essentially what paralegals do, and may be paid the same hourly rate. One of the advantages of having law clerks who are attending law school is that when they graduate, you may have a potential associate who will take time off to study for the bar exam, and if successful, return to your firm full-time. Your established relationship can be extremely productive for your business.

THE CONTRACT ATTORNEY

If you have a critical research problem that can make your case successful or not, you may not want to trust a law clerk or a paralegal. It may be advisable for you to hire a practicing lawyer just for a single legal research project. Research lawyers are not as easily located as paralegals and law clerks. They may be sole practitioners themselves, with a very limited advertising budget or exposure to the public. The networking that you have developed in your local bar association and civic organizations can often help you find a lawyer whose quality of work is acceptable to your colleagues, and to whom you can trust important things such as the core research for your case. A good place to look for such a lawyer is in the group that specializes in appellate court work. This is also a good way to get to know someone who can handle your appellate needs in the future.

This kind of arrangement may evolve over the years into a regular relationship. Such a lawyer may eventually join your firm with a specific function of providing legal research and appellate work. He or she may also have the ability to bring in individual work from the outside.

In all likelihood, you are not going to be hiring an associate immediately upon opening your start-up law firm, unless you have some experience in the practice of law and have enough clients to sustain the financial remuneration necessary for the firm to take off. That is why it is important to be careful in choosing contract attorneys and law clerks in the beginning—they may very well evolve into associates who you will take into the firm.

Paralegals do not necessarily fall into that category, because paralegals are defined as those people doing work under lawyers' supervision who are not necessarily on their pathway to becoming a lawyer. Some people who are very intelligent and adept at research and understanding legal concepts do not have the patience, the desire, or the finances to go through law school. Many of them are happily fulfilled doing work for lawyers and being an important part of a law firm.

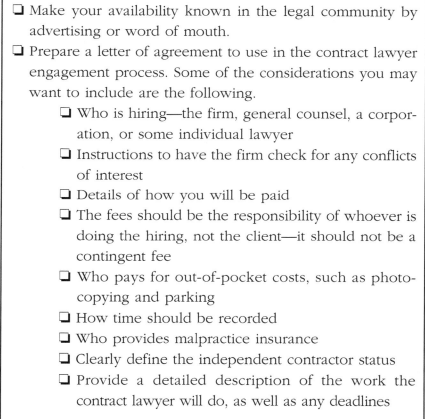

Contract Lawyer Checklist

❑ Make your availability known in the legal community by advertising or word of mouth.

❑ Prepare a letter of agreement to use in the contract lawyer engagement process. Some of the considerations you may want to include are the following.

   ❑ Who is hiring—the firm, general counsel, a corporation, or some individual lawyer

   ❑ Instructions to have the firm check for any conflicts of interest

   ❑ Details of how you will be paid

   ❑ The fees should be the responsibility of whoever is doing the hiring, not the client—it should not be a contingent fee

   ❑ Who pays for out-of-pocket costs, such as photo-copying and parking

   ❑ How time should be recorded

   ❑ Who provides malpractice insurance

   ❑ Clearly define the independent contractor status

   ❑ Provide a detailed description of the work the contract lawyer will do, as well as any deadlines

POLICIES AND PROCEDURES

As soon as you start making decisions about your firm's policies and procedures—and that should be early in the planning stages—begin creating manuals. They will grow along with your firm. Policies and procedures manuals promote the efficient operation of your office and enable new and temporary employees to function in the office with a minimum explanation. Every employee should get copies of your manuals and be notified of periodic updates.

Easily updated electronic manuals can be supplemented with samples of forms and other materials kept in a binder. One staff person, usually an office administrator, should be responsible for keeping the manuals current.

Policy Manual Checklist

❑ Confidentiality
❑ Attendance at meetings
❑ Respect for all persons
❑ Harassment issues
❑ Smoking
❑ Dress code and grooming
❑ Conduct and decorum
❑ Housekeeping
❑ Holiday observances
❑ Lines of authority

Procedure Manual Checklist

❑ Step-by-step guidelines for each task in the office
❑ Human resources issues
❑ Office hours
❑ Appointments, vacation, sick leave, and other time-off issues
❑ Overtime
❑ Leave of absence, maternity/paternity
❑ Bereavement
❑ Grievances, ombudsman, etc.
❑ Resignation, suspension, termination
❑ Harassment
❑ Working from home
❑ Job sharing
❑ Part-time employment

❏ Health insurance
❏ Time sheets, pay periods, other payroll issues
❏ Profit sharing
❏ Bonuses
❏ Training opportunities
❏ Statutes of limitation
❏ Conflict checking
❏ Calendaring and diary systems
❏ Indexing protocols for paper and electronic files
❏ Detailed description of new matter entry
❏ Computer logons
❏ Procedures for file backup
❏ Phone system
❏ Mail system, messengers, express services, logging deliveries
❏ Other equipment (photocopiers, printers, scanners, postage meters, etc.)
❏ Accounting, accounts payable, reimbursements, petty cash
❏ List and sample of all forms used in the office with current revision date
❏ Staff roster
❏ Frequently used numbers and emergency contact information, including courts, local bar association, temporary agencies, messenger services, contract services, computer technician, landlord, plumber, etc.
❏ Safety issues
❏ Emergency procedures, including location of first aid kit and Automatic Electronic Defibrillator (AED), CPR/AED instructions, and evacuation plan with map
❏ Federal and local government required postings for employees to view

chapter eight:
Outside Support Services

In addition to your office staff, your law practice will benefit from a professional relationship with a certified public accountant, a reliable insurance broker, a real estate broker, and a variety of other consultants.

As has been said earlier, a real estate broker is mandatory while looking for office space, particularly if you are going to be leasing. You should choose someone who is familiar with the geographical area, who has a reputation for being trust-worthy, and who you personally like.

Choosing an accountant is extremely important, because your law practice will function smoothly only if income, expenses, and other financial transactions are provided for in an orderly fashion. A *set of books* must be established for you, and there are accounting needs that will apply uniquely to the practice of law. For example, some jurisdictions require that trust accounts be established in a certain way. There are account-ants who know how to deal with this special requirement, and will advise you as to how to protect yourself from vio-lating any rules that are involved in such special trust accounts for clients' funds.

An insurance broker is an absolute necessity in setting up a law firm. Remember to keep nurturing your relationship with your bankers. They can keep you informed of financial programs that are constantly being developed by lending institutions.

FINDING TRUSTWORTHY CONSULTANTS

Experts and consultants may advertise in legal journals and newspapers, but this may not be the best place to seek expert help. Word of mouth is often the best way to locate trustworthy experts, including expert witnesses and other consultants. As you talk with other lawyers, you can ask for their recommendations for accountants, computer experts, and even interior designers. Ordinarily, lawyers are very helpful in this regard. Always check references.

Although it is not absolutely necessary, geographic proximity may be desirable in working with any of those professionals mentioned. You may want to have meetings and conferences in your office or theirs, and being close to one another can conserve time and reduce travel expenses.

ACCOUNTANTS

One of the most important choices to be made before opening your doors is obtaining the services of a good accountant who has experience in dealing with law firms. The accountant will be entrusted to set up the accounting system, the ledgers for each bank account, the accounting system for billing for each file, the systems for payroll deductions, and certainly, the accounting for your trust account. The most common disciplinary sanctions against beginning lawyers are caused by a commingling of a clients' funds with those of the attorney.

There are many accounting systems to choose from, and the accountant you engage will explain the value and unique feature of the ones you should consider. Make certain your accountant understands the requirements unique to each jurisdiction regarding the maintenance of client trust accounts and records of those accounts. Many jurisdictions have stringent rules, statutes, or regulations governing how client trust funds are to be handled. This is something that you must know and put into practice at the outset. If the accountant is learning how to deal with client's funds along with you, make certain that the rules and regulations of your jurisdiction are clear.

Banks will be very accommodating in helping you set up client trust accounts. They will have materials on how accounts should be monitored, and will help you and your accountant deal with this aspect of the practice. Additionally, banks can provide payroll withholding services for you, at a fee, and your accountant may urge you to avail yourself of that service. Your entire payroll can be handled by the bank, relieving you and your accountant of a cumbersome and expensive process. Your bank may do your payroll for you at little or no charge if you keep all of your deposits and loans with it.

Your accountant should make certain that you obtain the necessary SS-4 and SS-8 forms, which are the *Application for Employer Identification Number* and the *Determination of Employee Work Status for Purposes of Federal Employment*

Taxes Income Tax Withholding, respectively. These and the following should be discussed with your accountant:

- obtaining a tax ID number;
- setting up payroll process (with a bank or other service);
- furnishing monthly profit and loss statements;
- providing accounts receivable and accounts payable figures as needed, no less than quarterly; and,
- setting up special accounts for taxes, such as FICA, Social Security, Medicare, and quarterly payment schedules.

BANKS

Having a banker working with you is essential in starting up any business, particularly a professional practice that must be operated just like any other business. First, you want to establish a connection with a bank and develop a credit rating in a positive way. One of the ways of doing this is to borrow a small amount of money from the bank and pay it back promptly. You can speak candidly with your banker on how to do this.

Borrowing the money needed to start and run your law firm is almost a necessity. You will need money for payroll funds, equipment lease fees, and a variety of other expenses. Clients do not always pay their bills on time, and you need flexibility in your cash flow to cover necessities.

The banker can really help a new business and help keep established businesses running. A banker can help with issues of debt management, as well as other financial matters.

A few of the things that you should discuss with your banker on a relatively regular basis include the following:

- your written financial statement after obtaining it from your accountant;
- establishing a line of credit so that you can obtain funds quickly;
- the costs, if any, of having the bank provide you with your employee withholding and payroll services;
- the process of obtaining an ATM card; and,
- the possibility of consolidation of consumer loans, such as credit card or car payment loans, and even student loans. Some banks have programs dealing with these consolidation plans, and they may be favorable for you.

INSURANCE

Obtaining the services of a reliable insurance broker is crucial, not only to help you understand and obtain coverage, but also to help control the cost of the various types of policies you will need. Finding someone who truly has your interests at heart and your needs in mind may not be easy. You may need to talk to a few different agents and compare the information you are receiving about your insurance needs. A good broker knows that as you and your firm grow, your insurance needs develop, and more business flows to the broker. If that broker has treated you fairly and professionally, the relationship can last a long time and be mutually beneficial.

Insurance is available to cover nearly any event. However, being protected for anything and everything comes at a steep price. When making your insurance decisions, you must weigh the risks involved against the likelihood of the event. In every area there are disastrous emergencies that occur. It can be a hurricane, flood, fire, civil disturbance, earthquake, labor strike, or other event that has a catastrophic impact on your staff and your practice. When disasters occur, their effects may last for a long time, even months or years in the cases of hurricanes or major earthquakes.

Consider insurance coverage to provide for these emergencies. Flood insurance, earthquake insurance, and hurricane insurance can be extremely expensive, and you may not be able to afford these kinds of coverage. Your business interruption policy may not cover these emergencies, so this is an important part of your discussion with your insurance broker. Know where you are protected and where you are not. The welfare of your staff should always come first, and you should create a written emergency plan to protect office personnel, taking into account the disasters that are most likely in your geographical region.

The beginning law firm must have various forms of insurance coverage in place when the doors open. If the firm has full-time employees, or part-time employees who work a certain number of hours (depending on the jurisdiction), workers' compensation is required by law.

Professional liability, also known as malpractice insurance, is not only desirable, but mandatory in some jurisdictions. It is absolutely necessary from a practical standpoint.

Premises liability insurance is extremely important as well. Automobile liability insurance is also important. It protects you from liability when you and your staff are driving a vehicle in the course or the scope of employment.

With all of these liability areas covered, you can next consider the expense of other types of insurance that are not critical at the moment you open your doors, but become more and more critical as you develop your practice. Health, life, and disability insurance are in this category, along with accidental death and dismemberment coverage. There are also business-related types of insurance, such as a key-man life or disability policy that will provide for the overhead if an important lawyer in the firm becomes disabled or dies. In the business insurance policy that covers you for property damage, there should be a provision for business interruption insurance, and you should have document replacement insurance.

As a part of your business insurance, you would be well-advised to include coverage for employment practices liability. This covers liability for suits brought by employees for things such as sexual harassment and wrongful termination. There are even relatively new policies for liability associated with your website, advertising, and things of that kind.

The fidelity bond, which you should obtain for any employee handling money, is a vital part of your insurance package. An important element of protection from an insurance point of view is the umbrella policy of excess coverage protection that can be available over and above your personal liability, vehicle liability, and premises liability coverage.

This book is not the place to go into an extensive study of insurance types or your individual insurance needs. That is why it is extremely important that you obtain the services of an insurance broker who can guide you into the kinds of coverage you need. You may have to obtain a special broker to acquire professional liability coverage.

Coverage

Just as in the medical profession, changes are occurring in the public's willingness to sue lawyers. Both professions have become targets for lawsuits from disgruntled patients or clients, and insurance coverage protection is costly, but necessary.

This shift has also caused a change in the way coverage is triggered. Today, most malpractice insurance is what has come to be called *claims-made*. This is coverage that is triggered by the making of a claim against the lawyer by someone and reported to the company during the policy period. This is contrasted with the older form of *occurrence* coverage, where the date of the occurrence triggered coverage.

Because of the nature of claims-made coverage, you should have insurance that covers you even after the law practice has terminated. This is sometimes called *tail coverage*. If you conclude your practice by going into teaching, taking the bench, or otherwise terminating the practice of law, tail coverage is necessary, and your broker can explain it in better detail.

The American Bar Association section on Law Office Management or Small Firm Management can be extremely helpful in giving you sources to find which kind of malpractice insurance is best for you. There are also policies provided by the bar associations in many jurisdictions, and these should be examined carefully. They can be very helpful and can be quite economical, compared to insurance in the open market. There may be some group insurance benefits because of being insured through a bar association. The bar associations may have policies that include coverage that will make the package very economical for you.

Selecting Coverage

Review the costs of insurance very carefully, and weigh just as carefully the need for certain kinds of insurance and the insurance face amounts. There may be certain unique things that you are asked to retain as counsel. Consult with your insurance agent as to whether or not these items should be scheduled on your policy as a specific item to be insured. You do not want to face the liability of the loss of something unique and valuable to your client while in your custody.

Your needs should be discussed in detail with your insurance broker, and make your business decision based on those discussions. The following is a checklist of various types of coverage you may need.

Insurance Checklist

❑ Comprehensive general liability insurance
❑ Professional liability insurance
❑ Premises liability insurance
❑ Workers' compensation insurance
❑ Business interruption, particularly document reconstruction insurance
❑ Scheduled items

---

chapter nine:
The Library

A law library can be part of the décor in the law firm. Having shelves of handsomely bound legal volumes can lend substance and trustworthiness to the image of the law firm. While many of the usual library sources are on discs, DVDs, and other electronic means, making shelves of books unnecessary for legal research purposes, the look a library provides can be invaluable.

Quite often, the conference room—where meetings are held and depositions are taken—provides the ideal location for the law library. If you are a sole practitioner with no conference room, you may find the need for bookshelves in your own office. It makes the access to the volumes much easier and makes double use of the space.

Building a traditional, printed law library is less important when you are starting up in a location either near a law library or where you can share a law library. Nevertheless, it is always wise to have the latest volumes available for legal research, particularly in the jurisdiction and focus of your practice.

Printed libraries can be very expensive, particularly with the supplements that keep the volumes current. Office libraries are capital investments, and can be depreciated. A CPA or other tax advisor can be helpful as you make decisions about such purchases.

As you develop your law practice, it may become clear that a printed law library is desirable. Then you need to justify the need for building the library with the cost, which can be considerable. A law library is effective only to the extent that it is current. Keeping the supplements current and adding new volumes as the need arises becomes a large part of the expense of maintaining a library.

GETTING BOOKS

If you are a recent law school graduate, you may receive special discounts and other special deals in the purchase of books from legal book publishers. These are very attractive, and most of them are exceedingly worthwhile. However, you should balance your ability to pay with your desire for certain sets of volumes.

A judicious selection of books coupled with the publishers' discounts can make a big difference in your practice. Selecting fundamental publications, such as state law digests, summaries, and dictionaries of legal and standard nature, will form the heart of your beginning collection.

The purchase of used books can be helpful in saving money. When libraries are being broken up—such as when a law firm has decided to close down, a sole practitioner has passed away, or a branch of a law firm has closed down in a certain location—books will often become available at attractive prices. Also, when firms merge and they do not need duplicate volumes, some may be sold. One of the most important sources of the location of libraries that are being broken up is through the legal publishers' representatives with whom you have developed a good working relationship. Another source is the law librarian at a large firm.

For all lawyers, beginning or otherwise, it is helpful to have a working relationship with a major legal book publisher's representative who calls on you either in person, over the telephone, or on the Internet to keep track of your needs. It is important to establish this relationship rather quickly. You will be able to take advantage of book bargains much more rapidly by dealing with the people who are closest to the book market.

The local legal newspapers carry advertisements by law firms, book dealers, and other sources for used books. Keep in mind that a used set of books may not be able to become current by merely adding the latest supplements. For example, the gap between the supplements in the current volume and the supplement that you would be obligated to buy may be too large, and a newer set of the volumes would be advisable. Some sets print replacement volumes to incorporate the supplements, and you want to make sure that your set contains the most current set of printed volumes.

PLEADINGS

In addition to research tools, summaries, digests, and other technical resources, you should include a book of forms in your library that contains the basics necessary for a beginning practice. It is much easier to draft pleadings, such as complaints, answers, and demurrers, when you have a boilerplate form to get you started. Obviously, using boilerplate can be dangerous if it does not apply to your case. All of the pleadings that you prepare must conform to the allegations and the issues in the subject matter of the case.

It may sound amusing to caution you on these issues, but many times beginning lawyers draft pleadings that contain material totally irrelevant to the case in question. This often betrays their lack of experience, and gets them off on the wrong foot with the court and with opposing counsel.

Although it is not necessary to have copies of other counsel's pleadings as a part of your library, it can be extremely helpful to go to the local courthouse and obtain copies of successful pleadings in the cases similar to the ones that you are handling, and use those pleadings, in a tailored form, for your particular case. It saves a great deal of time and effort, especially for sole or duo practitioners who can benefit from the pleadings prepared by the mega firms. Pleadings are not copyrighted and become part of the public domain, and since all of the larger firms have pleading *banks* from which to draw, it is perfectly understandable for beginning lawyers from smaller firms to take advantage of the public records.

This is a situation where you want to make sure that a complaint has successfully survived the defendants' demurrers and motions to strike, the court has already ruled on the issues (from a pleading standpoint), and the complaint is viable. On rare occasions, you will find that the answers to complaints are subject to a demurrer, but in almost all cases, the answers will provide a good source of pleading examples for you if the cases are similar. Most public law libraries have forms and articles from publications for photocopying and augmenting your library.

In a practice that is essentially transactional, forms and printed guides are the lifeblood of the firm's work. A set of forms that is as complete as possible is required for you to do your work. These may be found in local law libraries or law school libraries and will suffice until you can obtain your own.

THE ELECTRONIC LAW LIBRARY

Increasingly, computer-assisted research is being made available to lawyers through LexisNexis, Jurisearch, Loislaw, FindLaw, and others. Law libraries, law schools, and large firms have these resources, and they can be made available to a beginning practitioner through their facilities. Law schools are providing training in operation of these services, and the services themselves provide training for the use of their systems. Computer-assisted services are helpful in finding specialized research or for supplemental research to make certain that the latest information is being used in your work.

These services are not free, and the cost for their usage can be substantial. The beginning practitioner may wish to contact public law libraries regarding their policies on the use of computer terminals and the fees for the charges for their services. In an office-sharing arrangement, the online services may be available and included in the rental cost, or may be billed separately.

One word of caution in the use of computer-assisted services: Long-term contracts for such services can be a burden.

The state of the art improves so rapidly you may be bound to a contract to use services that are becoming obsolete, and may not give you the competitive advantage you need for your case.

CD-ROM technology is not only replacing books, but is also making vast amounts of research material available to small firms and sole practitioner firms in a minimum amount of space. Entire state codes and treatises can be on CD-ROM, and the necessary updates, supplements, and access can be managed electronically and quite simply. More importantly, in areas where square foot rental costs are problematic, entire libraries can be maintained in a very small space.

PUBLICATIONS NEEDED

To list all of the publications that should be in a beginning law practice library would be well beyond the scope of this book, and is not necessary. There are several good sources for this information that would be applicable to your specific geographical area and type of practice. First, the local law library can be very helpful in assisting you in making a list of essential print and electronic library materials that you should have. Also available are the resources form the American Bar Association and local bar association sections pertaining to law office management, young lawyer services, and small firms.

This reinforces, once again, the importance of a beginning lawyer to connect with not only the law-related organizations, but civic organizations in the community as well. These organizations are advanced sources of networking contacts to help you determine what you should have in your library.

While you are discussing that subject, you may learn of lawyers who need contract services for court appearances, depositions, and other services that will help you augment your income as you get started. In the civic organizations, spread the word of your availability, and you can begin the acquisition of clients or augment the client base that you have already established.

As you get into your practice, you will modify the following list, but it does provide a basic starting point for any law library.

- *Black's Law Dictionary*
- Directory of local lawyers
- Standard English dictionary
- Basic form book for civil pleadings
- Summary of the law of the local law jurisdiction
- Federal resource materials, if your practice is substantially in the federal court system
- Specialty texts and forms if your specialty is very narrow, such as banking law, securities law, antitrust, or family law

chapter ten:
Financing

The most important element in beginning a law firm is having enough money to fund the necessary things for such an enterprise. Intuitively, this seems to be a catch-22 situation, because you have to have money to make money.

The understandable anxiety and depression experienced in the contemplation of financing a new law firm are not necessarily terminal. One of the best ways to reduce anxiety in any situation is to face the subject head-on and examine the options that are available to you. Rarely is there a situation in which a person has absolutely no options. By examining them, solutions can be found, personal tension can be reduced, and a vital step in professional success can be made.

RAISING CAPITAL

Essentially, there are several ways of raising the capital necessary to start a law firm. The first is by having money available through savings, gifts, or the sale of assets. Savings can come from the income of the partners, who are working in other positions, or from a married couple pooling their income to fund a share in a budding law firm. Gifts can come from family, such as parents or grandparents, and the sale of assets can occur under any number of circumstances. Selling assets can be a problematic way of raising funds, because the assets may be earning income and the choice of having income reduced creates a new catch-22.

If you are willing to devote a considerable amount of your practice time to charitable pro bono activities, you may want to explore the charitable foundations that make grants available to lawyers who want to spend time on worthwhile causes that would not receive lawyer's attention otherwise. Keep in mind, however, that whenever you are involved with the government and use its money, you must be willing to tolerate the irritation of having to do the paperwork. The government and charitable organizations must justify every penny that is spent, and since there is no profit involved, the only way the expenditure of the money can be traced and evaluated is through paperwork.

Beginning your law practice with outside money is good, if you can obtain your loan early in the process. That means that your own personal savings and other personal financial resources are held in reserve for those instances when you may need to take hold of an opportunity on equipment that must be acted upon immediately.

This money can come from personal credit of the sole practitioner and the family involved, or the potential partners or shareholders and their families. Banks will often take a first or second mortgage on real property to provide funds for establishing a new law firm. The *Small Business Administration* has a loan guarantee program and Direct

Loan Programs, and these avenues should be explored if all of the traditional sources of financing are unavailable.

Another form of credit is *accounts receivable*. Frequently, when a new law firm is being created, the creators already have been in practice and have clients on a regular basis. This provides not only an attractive asset for a bank, but may provide actual accounts receivable. This can be the basis for a working capital loan or, under certain circumstances, factored in order to raise the capital.

Factoring is a very expensive way to raise funds in which the lender becomes the payee for the client and the money is paid directly to the factor, who then undertakes the responsibility for collecting the money. For a law firm, this is the least favorable way of financing a firm and is not recommended. This kind of financing is more common in businesses involving products rather than services.

DEBT MANAGEMENT

If financing is the most singularly important element in beginning the law firm, then debt management is the most singularly important factor in keeping the firm financially viable. Regardless of the source of the start-up money, you should accept the fact that over the years of a law practice, it is going to be necessary to have a good credit rating and a stable line of credit. Debt and borrowing is a necessary part of any business—especially a personal service business, such as a law practice. Consequently, it is imperative that you develop a relationship with a bank before you begin the first step toward acquiring financing.

You must keep a close and continual relationship with your personal banker. It is advisable to have a regular time to meet for lunch either quarterly or on whatever schedule seems reasonable for you both. You will want your accountant to prepare financial statements for your banker on a regular basis if you have outstanding loans. They may be the subject of your meetings. Your banker may suggest someone who will be your financial advisor, not only for the firm, but also for you personally.

Debt management is something that changes constantly, because your accounts payable and accounts receivable change constantly. Ask your accountant or your bookkeeper to provide you with frequent profit and loss statements that include the accounts payable and accounts receivable figures. You may even want a very quick statement of the total accounts receivable and accounts payable only.

Keep in mind the normal collectible percentage of your accounts receivable. There are always going to be amounts that are uncollectible, and they generally form a predictable percentage of your accounts. Factor that percentage into the total figure you have, and you can give yourself an educated estimate of how much potential income as contrasted with the amount of short-term debt that you must pay.

Remember, work closely with your accountant and your banker if you see that your debt is getting to a point where it is going to be a problem. Insolvency, bankruptcy, or other financial crisis can be avoided if you pay attention to your debt management.

Dealing with Student Loans

Many of today's law school graduates start their careers with six-figure debt. Even with scholarships and grants, loan obligations can far exceed what a new lawyer might hope to earn in annual salary. Unfortunately, compounding interest means that debt becomes more expensive as it lingers unpaid. Repayment periods stretch out over ten, twenty, or thirty years. Outstanding student loans can interfere with your ability to secure the business loans necessary to establish your practice.

Most student loans allow a six-month grace period after graduation before repayment must begin. Some lenders will defer (but not forgive) payments for other reasons. Some institutions may forgive student loans for graduates who go into public service or have family emergencies that take them out of practice. The best plan, however, is to assume that you will have to repay your loan and to establish a repayment system as soon as possible. Simply making the monthly payment that appears on your statement may not be the best approach to your indebtedness. Consider some of the variables that can affect the balance and options for meeting your obligation.

- *Interest rate.* While the principal balance ticks downward ever so slowly, the interest on that balance continues to compound. Depending upon current market conditions, switching from a variable rate to a fixed rate of interest may reduce the overall cost of your loan.
- *Loan consolidation.* You may be repaying several loans, which were issued at several different rates of interest, and making multiple payments each month. Consolidating these loans may enable you

to secure a lower interest rate, but always measure such monthly savings against the total repayment cost for the life of the loan, which may be extended to thirty years.

- *Begin paying before you graduate.* In some cases, students can consolidate their loans and begin repayment at lower student rates while they are still in school, saving substantially on the lifetime cost of borrowing.

- *Special payment plans.* You may be able to structure or restructure your loan so that your payments gradually increase or are specifically tied to your income.

- *Repay sooner rather than later.* The sooner you can repay your loans, the less they will cost you. For example, a $60,000 loan at 4% interest will cost approximately $73,000 if paid off in ten years, but more than $103,000 if paid off over thirty years.

- *Check for early payment penalties.* As you become more successful, you may find yourself with a large influx of cash. If your loan allows early payments without penalty, consider paying down a substantial portion of your loan in addition to your usual monthly payment. Even adding $50 to your payment each month can significantly reduce the cost of your loan.

- *Talk with your lender.* The lender has every reason to want you to fulfill your repayment obligations. If you default on your loan, the lender loses money. If you find yourself in a bind, talk with your lender or loan servicer as soon as possible. Do not wait until the warning notices and phone calls start arriving. By showing your intent to pay, you may find the lender more willing to accommodate you with a temporary reprieve or a reduced payment amount. Such accommodations are known as *forbearance.*

- *Talk with your family.* Family members may be willing to help you by paying off a portion or all of your outstanding loans and structuring a repayment schedule at a lower interest rate. Reducing your interest rate by a point, a half-point, or even a quarter-point can save you thousands of dollars over the life of the loan. A family member may even be willing to defer repayment for five years to allow you to establish your practice and build your client base and income.

You will undoubtedly be contacted by an assortment of lenders and loan servicers who are eager to help you manage your debt. By all means, consult a trusted financial advisor before changing the way you deal with your student loans. Some bar associations have what they call Student Loan Consolidation Program. This enables anyone with more than a certain amount, usually $7,500, in outstanding federal student loans to reduce monthly loan payments and lock in at the lowest interest rate in many years. These programs can make available a Federal Consolidation Loan, which is part of the group of loans available under the *Federal Family Education Loan* (FFEL) program as authorized by the federal government. The Federal Consolidation Loan program was established by Congress to help student borrowers manage the burden of federal student loan debts.

With such a loan, you can combine all or some of your outstanding loans into a single one, even if the loans are currently held by more than one member and are of different types. Such consolidation allows a choice of flexible repayment terms and then fix low interest rates for the rest of the life of the loan. Not only do you save on the lower interest rate, but you can also save an additional .60% if you consolidate your loans within your grace period (the period after you graduate and before you begin repaying your loans). You may consolidate any of the loans listed below, but only if you are combining a loan with at least one other eligible loan.

- Federal Stafford Loans, unsubsidized and subsidized (including Guaranteed Student Loans/GSL)
- Direct Stafford Loans, unsubsidized and subsidized
- Federal Supplemental Loans for Student (formerly Auxiliary Loans to Assist Students/ALAS and Student Plus Loans)
- Federal Perkins Loans, formerly National Defense/National Direct Student Loans (NDSL)
- Health Professions Student Loans, including loans for Disadvantaged Students (HPLS)
- Federal Insured Student Loans (FISL)
- Federal PLUS (Parent Loans)
- Direct PLUS Loans
- Federal Consolidation Loans, unsubsidized and subsidized
- Direct Consolidation Loans, unsubsidized and subsidized
- Nursing Student Loans (NSL)

For information with respect to loan consolidation, you should contact a loan counselor at your school, bar association, or other organization with whom you may be dealing regarding student loans. By extending your loan term and selecting a repayment plan by way of consolidation, you may lower your monthly payments by as much as 50%. You should also remember that there is no penalty for early repayment of your consolidated loan, so you may pay them off at any time or simply make higher payments when you are able to do so. Also, remember that by extending the time, you are possibly creating an increase in your financial obligation because you will be making payments for a longer period of time, both principle plus interest.

The federal government regulates how the fixed interest rate is determined on your consolidation loan. For additional and detailed information on the advantages of consolidation and the payments required, you should contact the loan counselor at the institutions previously mentioned.

Your decisions and actions regarding your indebtedness can affect your business for years. Do not default on your loans. Be sure to make payments on time. Keep thorough and accurate records of payments. If you meet or speak with your lender, loan servicer, or financial advisor about your debt, keep a record of the date, the name of the person you spoke with, and the topics covered in your discussion. It is always a good idea to follow up such conversations with a letter that confirms any agreements or decisions that were made. Let your lender know immediately if you move or change your bank account or contact information.

When you are starting your practice, your outstanding student loans may seem an insurmountable obstacle to success. By establishing a reasonable repayment program, developing and following a practical budget, and working steadily toward your personal and professional goals, you will soon find yourself able to repay your loans and to make more profitable use of the money you work so hard to earn.

BUDGET

In the ideal world, when you begin your practice, it is nice to have enough money to provide the furniture, equipment, supplies, and staff expenses for six to eight months. This will give you a minimal amount of time to send out a billing and receive money from your accounts receivable. Remember, you also have personal expenses and costs to take care of in that same period of time, and provisions must be made for both business and personal needs.

One of the ways to minimize or even eliminate the stress of the unknown in start-up costs is to begin a rough budget of your monthly needs, even using estimates, and multiply them by six or eight months. That will give you the amount of start-up money that you should be looking for. A few phone calls will give you the monthly estimates for rent, equipment leasing, furniture leasing, and contract services for staff or contract lawyers. Simple office supplies can be easily estimated and included in this rough budget. A total of these expenses will give you a realistic estimate of what you will need to begin. Suddenly, the anxiety of the unknown is reduced because you now have rational parameters to work within.

Your rough budget should be in two basic parts. The first part is the start-up costs, which will occur only once, such as buying furniture. The second part of such a budget should contain expense items and income items. The income, of course, must be an estimate, but it is quite feasible to estimate the income if you are doing work where you bill clients by the hour and you have an approximation of how much work you will be doing in the first six to eight months of the practice.

CASH FLOW

Another important aspect of operating a small business, such as a beginning law firm, is keeping cash flow as regular as possible. That million-dollar case really does you no good if you cannot keep your doors open for the two years it takes to get a verdict. Maintaining a regular and predictable amount of money coming in and going out is key.

There are natural ebbs and flows in a business cycle. A loan from a bank may be necessary to smooth out these peaks and valleys. However, there are often creative ways to handle cash flow issues that do not involve loans or letting bills stack up. You simply have to think outside of the box and ask the right questions, as the following example illustrates.

Example

A young lawyer began a law firm, bringing several clients with him when he left a larger firm. After the new law firm was established, a very significant client (in terms of total revenue) announced that all of the files be billed every six months, rather than monthly. Because the lawyer had a substantial number of files for that client, he went to his banker to inquire how he could work out a line of credit to take care of six months' worth of expenses attributable to that significant number of files for that client.

His banker asked him if this billing requirement was for all of the cases of this client at the same time or for each individual case. The lawyer had not thought to ask that question, and the banker said that she thought it was a crucial question for him to have asked his client because there were ways of working out a solution to the cash flow problem without borrowing at all.

The young lawyer went back to the client and learned that he was to be billed every six months in each individual file. The lawyer then instructed the bookkeeper for the firm to look at the billing history of the files for that client and separate them into six groups, with each group to be billed every six months, but one group to be billed every month, so that when the last of the group had been billed, they could start the cycle over again. The client was happy because the firm was, in effect, bankrolling a good deal of the expense and time involved, and the firm was happy because their monthly cash flow was coming into the firm's coffers.

Section Two:
Managing Your Law Office

chapter eleven:
The Organized Office

Having a computerized office system makes it imperative that you establish a system not only for calendaring, but opening, indexing, and cross-indexing your files, as well as other pertinent information that you will need outside of the file, such as the category. Setting up future calendar dates for the file is also advisable. A computerized diary and a written diary are absolutely essential in starting up a law firm.

INDEXING

In beginning an office network, an index protocol should be established immediately. All persons with access to the network must follow the protocol, so that documents of a recurring nature and documents that pertain to particular projects will be identified and filed where all users of the system can retrieve them easily. For example, all cases can be stored in one drive on the computer and all non-case-related office information stored in another. Within the case directories, standard designations for pleadings, discovery, correspondence, attorney notes, and the like should be established.

Use of subdirectories for frequently accessed items, such as research memoranda, deposition summaries, interview notes, deposition preparation notes, pleadings, and documents related exclusively to trial, will also save considerable time as more people begin using the system and adding documents to it. Administrative documents should be filed by major categories in subdirectories. For example, documents related to office administration could go in a subdirectory entitled "administration" or "office," and practice guides, such as sample memoranda, research sources, and pattern discovery, can go in a separate subdirectory.

The key to effective storage and retrieval of documents is uniformity in naming the files. If a particular system user has a favorite method of identifying documents, and this is not readily apparent to other users, the document may effectively be lost to other system users. File identification standards should be established immediately as part of the index protocol.

SETTING UP THE FILE

The first document to go into the new file is the case memorandum resulting from the client interview. This should include any notes, photographs, drawings, or anything else that has been used in the interview to describe or set out the matters for which representation has been agreed. A new file should contain all of the essential information necessary to maintain contact with the client, such as name, addresses, telephone and cell phone numbers, email addresses, websites, and any other means of obtaining information about the client and maintaining communication.

In intellectual property cases, manuscripts, models, or drawings may be included in the file.

After the engagement as counsel is accepted and the file has been opened and entered into the system, it is important, as a high quality law practice, to prepare an *Initial Memorandum to the File.* This is a source of information not only to refresh your memory, but to guide those who work on the file with you, as well as anyone who might work on the file if you are rendered unable to handle the matter for any reason. The client's interests are kept uppermost when all of the pertinent information is in the file. The Memorandum should contain all transactional deadlines and details.

In the Memorandum, you want to set out the case strategy, which contains the client's goals, the necessary discovery, expert witnesses, jury instructions, and even ideas for a closing argument for trial. It should also include the pertinent deadlines that are involved. For example, federal courts require very stringent adherence to deadlines for case management purposes. Some statutes of limitation are as long as five or ten years. Tort deadlines, government claims deadlines, and other critical limitations should be noted in the file and entered into the computerized diary and calendaring systems.

Some state courts have rules that are difficult to follow. These are to be noted for the file. Next, isolate the serious problems that you have seen in your client's case. Identify documents, witnesses, or other considerations that can be particularly dangerous or detrimental to your client's case. Part of the problem in the case may be the expense necessary to pursue the matter. A rough budget should be set out to give you and your client some idea of the financial implications of legal action.

Redundancy can be extremely valuable in maintaining files. Damage to the computer and its data would have disastrous effects not only on the law firm, but also on the clients. It is absolutely critical to have a backup system for computer data.

Not only is safety an important factor for your client, but you want them to feel comfortable and trusting in their relationship with you and your firm. The documentation that they are given at the beginning is critical to the feeling of well-being that you want to create.

Included here are some suggested forms for you to use at the outset of your clients contact. You may modify them to suit your individual needs, particularly if you specialize in any particular kind of practice.

Client Interview Form

1. Who recommended the client to you? _____

    a. Make a conflicts check regarding the recommender:

    _____

    b. Send thank you note to the recommender, if you are engaged: _____

2. Make detailed notes of the matter using attached sheets of paper, which may be necessary: _____

_____

3. Obtain all telephone numbers, email addresses, next of kin, person to notify in emergency, or any other information necessary for communications: _____

_____

4. If the matter involves personal injury or property damage, obtain all insurance policies pertaining to your client: ____

_____

5. If the matter is a business dispute, obtain all documents, names and addresses of those involved, and estimated monetary losses: _____

_____

6. If the matter is a will or a trust, obtain the name, address, and telephone number of the client's tax advisor, all legatees or beneficiaries, spouse, children, and parents, if applicable:

_____

_____

continued

7. If the client's business is involved in any matter of any kind, give the client your Tax ID number for purposes of their records, and you obtain their Tax ID number for your records: _____

8. If the matter is a criminal one, in addition to the information contained in the telephone contact, keep in mind that your fee must be determined and paid at the outset of the representation: _____

9. After confirming client's engagement of your firm, review each paragraph of the engagement letter, preferably in the presence of a secretary, paralegal, or other staff, whose name should be noted: _____

_____

10. The client should take the copy, and at least go to a separate room, discuss it with whomever accompanied the client, sign it, and return it.

Authority to Release Records

TO WHOM IT MAY CONCERN:

The undersigned hereby gives you the authority to furnish to my attorneys _____ [Firm Name] or their representatives all records, documents, papers, recordings, and all other things, such as medical records, including but not limited to charts, X-rays, laboratory reports, electronically recorded data, MRI, or CT scan records, and all other things pertaining to my accident, which occurred on or about _____, 20_____, in or about _____ [city], _____ [state].

Date: _____

Signed: _____ [Client]

_____ [Guardian Ad Litem]

_____ [Attorney in Fact]

Case Memorandum

Date: _____   Statute of Limitations:_____

File No: _____

Potential Adversaries:

Client:

Witness:

Documents:

Facts:

Strategies:

Pertinent Legal Authorities:

    Statutes:

    Cases:

RETAINER AGREEMENTS

At the initial interview with the client, some form of written notation of the session should be made. It is just as important to set up the terms of the retainer as it is to fill out the terms of the non-retainer.

The interests of the attorney and the client are best protected by a written record of what transpired. One of the most infuriating dilemmas for an attorney is to be faced with a malpractice lawsuit with no written information about the interview or conversation, while the *client* is able to testify under oath (and quite effectively) that there definitely was an attorney/client relationship when the lawyer was interviewed.

Another danger is when someone does not become a client, and the attorney should have advised that person of some critical information that was clearly evident. For example, if the statute of limitations is involved and the attorney did not mention it or advise a non-client of the problem, a case may be made for legal malpractice even though the attorney was never effectively retained.

Such obvious issues as statute of limitations are not necessarily the only basis for such potential malpractice. Subtle issues of antitrust implications, government tort claims act regulations, and other things may be raised against the lawyer. Information of that kind should be established in the retainer interview, and the wording should state clearly that no attorney/client relationship was established, and the non-client was advised to seek legal assistance immediately with respect to statute of limitations and other potentially important issues.

One of the pitfalls to avoid is that of having multiple clients present at the retainer meeting. Family matters, business matters in a small family-owned business, and other situations of that kind can be dangerous for the attorney and for the client, as well as the non-client. The conflict of interest that can arise in a multiple-party interview or retainer meeting must be thought about very carefully, and the parties should be given the opportunity to retain independent counsel.

This becomes critical when the attorney is involved in a business deal with clients, and the retainer meeting coincides with the formation of the business, either corporate, partnership, or otherwise. If you enter into a business-related activity with your client or clients, and you perceive that a conflict has arisen or may arise, it is not sufficient for you to tell them that a conflict has arisen and they should seek independent counsel. To avoid malpractice, you must give the factual basis for the conflict in order for them to make proper choices and decisions. If they think that the conflict is slight, they may not seek counsel. Problems for the attorney are particularly serious in each conflict or potential conflict, and must be determined and resolved as quickly as possible.

A written waiver of conflict can be obtained, but independent legal advice for the parties involved in the conflict is necessary most of the time. This way the waiver is made knowingly and all of the parties are made aware of the realities of the conflict.

Many jurisdictions require written retainer agreements between counsel and clients, and most of them require specific information to be contained within these agreements. The matter for which the attorney has been retained and the scope of the attorney's work should be described with as much detail as possible. Regardless of whether or not the jurisdiction requires a retainer agreement, it is the best practice to have one.

CALENDARING

The process of taking in clients' cases through the process of engagement, opening a file, performing the legal services, and then storing the file is a metamorphosis that must be carefully established, calendared, and monitored. It is absolutely imperative that a strong calendar control system is in place from the beginning.

While the necessity for calendar control is obvious in a litigation firm, the need for calendaring is equally imperative in a transactional law firm. Deadlines for the drafting of documents, meetings with clients, meetings with other lawyers, meetings with experts and specialists, appearances in court, depositions, due dates for interrogatories and other discovery, pleading dates, responses to discovery, tax deadlines, and crucial data pertaining to securities and other information must be kept in the firm's calendar for review and control. The standard practice in all jurisdictions requires precise recording of these important matters. There is little, if any, margin for error, and no excuse for sloppiness of any kind.

Your calendaring system should have redundancies and be able to span more than just a one-year period. In addition to the firm calendar, each lawyer should have a personal calendar repeating the same information as the master one. Also, a statute book, which contains the statutes of limitations applicable, should be kept for each file. Since court dates or other meetings can be scheduled many months in advance, the calendar must be able to accommodate future dates beyond the end of any given year.

For office calendars and personal calendars, there are many systems available at office supply stores, legal book stores, and stationery stores. It is important that you find one that is comfortable and practical for you. If a system is tedious or cumbersome, you may avoid using it and miss recording pertinent information.

Leaving out important dates with the intention of putting them in at a later time is dangerous. As awkward as it may seem, calendar dates should be entered immediately. The time required to enter them is minimal, and if not handled immediately, the likelihood that they will be forgotten or missed is high.

Develop a habit of going over the office calendar on a certain day at a certain time every week. As soon as you open the doors of your new firm, it is good office practice to have a calendar conference weekly with those involved in the firm—even if there are only two of you. Office and personal calendars should be coordinated and details confirmed. As the firm grows in staff and in lawyers, this becomes part of the culture, and it will save the firm from disaster time and time again.

If the calendar conference is time-consuming, it can be scheduled for lunchtime, and the firm can bring in sandwiches for a working lunch. This does not intrude on the lawyer's billable time, and at the same time, staff get to have a paid lunch. They also now have free time after the calendar conference to get the errands done that they would have done normally during their lunch break.

Conducting this calendar conference serves as a good way to discover weaknesses in the system and who is procrastinating, not meeting deadlines, or otherwise in need of some counseling in order to keep the law office running smoothly.

The key element in the calendaring system is having someone with the personal responsibility of maintaining the firm's calendar and making all of the entries in the calendar. The calendar is only as good as the information provided to the person responsible for it, so the firm must have a standard system of data entry for the calendar.

To get information into the calendar, attorneys, assistants, paralegals, and all staff members must follow the same system. Regardless of what system you choose for your office, there should be one system, and it should be oriented toward getting the information quickly and accurately into the calendar.

Many law firms prepare their own forms that contain all the information necessary for the calendar entry, such as the name of the attorney, the date in question, the nature of the entry (such as department and court for an appearance, or the location of a deposition), and the case name involved. These forms should be collected at the end of the work day and given to the person responsible for the calendar and entered immediately.

Some law office management software contains calendaring procedures that can be done from the various stations in the office network. A special folder is established in the computer system just for calendaring. Data is keyed into the computer, and then automatically entered into the appropriate date and category on the calendar. In this way, anyone in the firm can go to the calendar folders and see in advance what is pertinent for each day. The firm and the individual attorney have a record that can be printed, thus giving a permanent record of what is on the calendar.

Calendar entries can be made outside the office via laptops and handheld computers, thus giving the firm a great deal of flexibility. An attorney can check the calendar using these devices from home or in an airplane. The calendar conference can be held via the Internet, and attorneys who are out of town can participate.

Each attorney has a separate calendar that is integrated into the centralized office calendar. This gives a backup to individual attorneys, the staff, and the firm. When an attorney is unavailable for calendar conferences or data entry, the attorney's secretary or assistant should be available to provide the information. The secretary or lawyer's assistant should have a separate calendar as well, which is a duplicate of the attorney's.

Paralegals and law clerks who are assigned to a specific case, lawyer, group of lawyers, or department, should also maintain the pertinent calendar. The paralegal is thus a part of the legal team, and the work gets done smoothly and efficiently because everyone is aware of the same deadlines and need for certain work to be completed.

The office calendar is so critical that it must be protected. At the end of the day, the master office calendar should be placed in a fireproof safe or file cabinet for protection, and the electronic version should be backed up. The calendar may be kept in a file on a computer and computer network, but it is still a good idea to have a manual master calendar that can serve as a backup for the computer system in case there is a technical problem.

DIARIES

Just as important as maintaining a calendar system is maintaining a diary system. Cases and files must be attended to, and the way to bring the file to the attorney's attention is by setting up a diary. For example, the calendar has the date for a meeting with the client, and the diary has a date for the file to be pulled for the attorney to study ahead of time. Secretaries, assistants, and other staff assigned to an attorney have the responsibility of maintaining the diary. This can take the form of a separate calendar. Each date is reviewed two days ahead, with the files pulled and made available to the attorney ahead of time.

Whether by software or manually, a *Daily Entry Slip* can contain diary dates, calendar dates, and the daily time sheet. A diary memo form is one of the most efficient ways to maintain a diary system. The diary memo serves at least two functions:
1. bringing up the file for review and
2. giving the attorney the immediate opportunity to write up in reasonable detail what was done on the file on that date and by whom.

The diary memo may also contain a space for purposes such as recording the billable work that was done, and is also a backup method for keeping time sheets. The secretary or assistant should enter the diary memos every day and make sure that the files are made available to the attorney.

Included at the end of the chapter are two forms for office management. One of the forms, the *Daily Entry Slip*, is included for your reference. In it, you can combine many types of information on one slip that can be given to the person who has the responsibility for collecting all of the data and recording it in the various, respective locations.

Statute Book

You should have a one-year, two-year, five-year, and ten-year diary or calendar system, so that statutes of limitations can be recorded for actions. The review of the statute book is important. The statute book is the responsibility of the firm, and the firm's calendar guardian should also be responsible for the statute book. The entries in the statute book are the personal responsibility of the attorney involved. This begins with the retainer meeting, and is subject to review every year, just to make sure that the dates relating to statutes of limitation are entered into the office calendar at the appropriate time. This becomes especially important when minors are involved in litigation or potential litigation.

The system of diary entries can be part of a software system, and the person assisting the attorney can bring up very quickly and see at a glance what files need to be pulled for that day, or even two days, in advance.

File Inventory

The file inventory in a law firm is one of the most neglected parts of the law office system, and it should not be. A file inventory, and an inventory and review of the statute book, should take place once a year. The best time for these tasks is the slowest time of year, often during a holiday season, when there is extra time to spend on something that is nonproductive in terms of income but vital to the health of the firm.

The files should be examined to make sure that there is a diary or callback date on each file, that there is a current status report to the client in the file, and that no deadline has been missed and no statute of limitation about to lapse.

Taking inventory of all the files in the office can be a daunting and laborious process. The most effective system is to divide the work up and assign teams to the various sections. It makes sense to use teams who are involved with that particular category of file, if possible. It may be a good idea to have a party to celebrate at the end of the annual file inventory.

Last but not least, part of the file inventory is an indication of whether the billing is current for that file, and if not, it should be brought up-to-date as quickly as possible.

EVIDENCE

A client may leave property or exhibits and other physical items in the custody of the firm. These things must be accounted for with as much detail as monetary deposits. They should be stored securely, and a written ledger of exhibits and physical property should be maintained with the case number and the date of the deposit, as well as any due date that may be required. Typically, five years after a matter has been closed, the files are destroyed. At that time, these physical properties should be inventoried and a determination made as to whether they should be destroyed or returned to the client.

Daily Entry Slip
[Name of firm]

Date: _____   Name: _____

Diary Dates:

File #s	Date:	File #s	Date:
_____	_____	_____	_____
_____	_____	_____	_____
_____	_____	_____	_____

Calendar Dates:

File #s   Date:

_____   _____   _____[depo.]
_____   _____   _____[trial]
_____   _____   _____[depo.]

Miscellaneous Dates:

_____   _____[vac.]
_____   _____[conf.]

Name of Assistant: _____
[person responsible to collect slips]

File #	Description	Hourly Rate	Time

Costs: File #s   Description
_____   _____[photocopying] $_____
_____   _____[parking] $_____
_____   _____[client lunch] $_____
_____   _____[mileage] $_____
_____   _____[etc.] $_____

Notes:

File Inventory Form

File Number: _____   Date: _____

Client: _____

Date:

      Last billing: _____

      Last letter to client: _____

      Last activity: _____

      Next scheduled activity: _____

      Next diary date: _____

Date file closed: _____

Suggestions:

[attach additional pages if necessary]

chapter twelve:
Billing and Fees

Clients are very happy to have you as a lawyer when they are in trouble. Quite often, they are effusive in their praise for you in the work that you do for them. There is sometimes a change in attitude when they receive the bill for your services. Consequently, your billing must be specific as to what you have done, and it must contain as much detail as practicable to educate your clients as to what you have done. An explanation to your clients through the billing process is the best possible way to educate them and to justify your billing and promote marketing for your firm.

This process begins with the initial contact with your client, including the fee agreement. It should be explained in detail to a client and should contain a provision for mediation first, then arbitration for any disputes relating to your relationship as attorney and client.

FEE AGREEMENT

At the initial interview, however informal it may be, you should discuss legal fees, costs, and expenses, and reach an agreement with the client as to these matters. A precise under-standing of the means for your compensation is essential—not only for the client, but for you. If the fee arrangement is not reached before representation begins, both client and attorney are risking financial loss, damage to the relationship, dissatis-faction, and perhaps even a professional liability lawsuit.

Keep in mind that it is dangerous to file a lawsuit for fees, because it inevitably draws a cross-complaint for malpractice. Moreover, if the fee agreement is not drafted relatively metic-ulously, any ambiguities that may arise are construed against you as the attorney, and all equitable options may be decided in the client's favor. Frequently, the client has very little nego-tiation as to the terms or fees in your legal representation. Consequently, those equitable duties *adhere* to you, in favor of the client.

Many jurisdictions require the fee agreement to be in written form. It is strongly recommended that if there is no such requirement the agreement should still be in writing.

A suggested *Fee Agreement* is set out here for you on the following pages.

Suggested Components of Fee Agreement

[Firm letterhead]

Legal Services Fee Agreement:

_____

[on behalf of the law firm of _____]

[Address: _____]
[_____]

_____("Attorney")
will provide legal services to _____
("Client") on the following conditions set forth herein.

Client engages Attorney to provide legal services in the following described matter: _____

_____

If a court action is required, Attorney will represent Client through trial and posttrial motions. This agreement does not cover representation for any appeals or proceedings after judgment. Separate agreement must be made for such services. Attorney will provide such legal services reasonably required to represent Client and will make reasonable efforts to keep Client informed of the status of the matter and to respond to Client's inquiries.

Client agrees to cooperate with Attorney, to keep Attorney informed of any developments related to the above described matter, and to be truthful with Attorney and abide by this agreement. Client agrees to pay Attorney's bills on time, and to keep Attorney advised of Client's current

continued

address, telephone number(s), and email address, if any. Client will provide Attorney necessary documents and information when requested and will appear when necessary at legal proceedings as required by Attorney.

Client agrees to make an initial retainer deposit of $_____ by _____, 20____. The hourly charges will be made against the deposit, which will be held in a trust account. Client hereby authorizes Attorney to pay fees and charges from said fund as they incur. Payments from that fund will be made upon Client's receipt of a billing statement. Client agrees that the deposit is not an estimate of total costs and is only an advance for them.

When the retainer is exhausted, Attorney reserves the right to require further deposits each up to $_____.

When a trial, or arbitration date, is set, Client should pay all sums due, and deposit the Attorney's fees estimated for preparation and completion of the trial, or arbitration, as well as jury fees, or arbitration fees, expert fees, and other costs, which are likely to be assessed, such funds may exceed the maximum amount of deposit.

Client agrees to pay an hourly fee at Attorney's prevailing rates for the time spent on Client's matters by Attorney's law firm. The current hourly rates charged are:

1. Senior Attorneys: $____/hr.
2. Partner Attorneys: $____/hr.
3. Associate Attorneys: $____/hr.
4. Paralegals: $____/hr.
5. Law clerks: $____/hr.

Attorney's rates are subject to change on a thirty-day written notice to Client. If Client declines to pay the new rates, Attorney will have the right to withdraw and terminate the Attorney/Client relationship.

The charges by Attorney will include time spent on telephone calls relating to Client's matter, including calls with Client. Other legal personnel assigned by Attorney to handle Client's matters, may confer among themselves as required and appropriate for the matter. When they confer, each person will charge for the work done and expended, which is reasonably related to the matter, and will not be any duplication. This will include attendance at meetings and legal proceedings. Attorney will charge for travel time and waiting time in court, and other proceedings. Time will be charged in a minimum unit of 0.1 hour.

Attorney will incur costs and expenses in performing legal services given including, but not limited to, service of process, filing fees, court and deposition reporter fees, jury fees, notary public fees, deposition costs, long-distance telephone charges, messenger and other related fees, postage, photocopying and other reproduction costs, travel costs, including parking, mileage, transportation, meals and hotel costs, investigation expenses, consultant fees, expert witness, professional, mediated, arbitrated and special master fees, and other items, for which Client agrees to pay, in addition to Attorney's hourly fee.

Attorney will charge:

$_____ for in-house photocopying per page
$_____ for facsimile charge
$_____ for travel time

continued

Client acknowledges that if the matter is involved in a court action or arbitration, the court or arbitrators may require Client to pay fees and the cost to other parties in the action. Such payments will be entirely the responsibility of Client.

Attorney will send the Client regular statements for fees and costs, each statement will be payable on receipt. However, Client may request a statement of intervals no less than thirty days. If Client requests one to be made available, Attorney will provide one within ten days. The statements shall include the rate, amount, and basis of calculation of the methods for determination of the fees and costs, each of which shall be clearly identified.

Attorney is hereby granted a lien by Client on any claims or causes of action that are the subject of this agreement. The lien will be for any sums owed to Attorney at the conclusion of services performed. The lien will attach to any recovery Client may receive either by arbitration, or judgment, settlement, or otherwise.

Client may discharge Attorney at any time. Attorney may withdraw with Client's consent or for good cause. Included in good cause are Client's breach of this agreement, refusing to cooperate with or follow Attorney's advice on a material matter involved in the case, or that would render Attorney's representation unlawful or unethical. When Attorney's services are terminated, all unpaid charges will become due and payable.

After services are terminated, attorney will, upon Client's request, deliver Client's file and property in Attorney's possession, whether or not Client has paid for all services.

Nothing in this agreement, and nothing in Attorney's statements to Client, will be construed as a promise or guarantee about the outcome of the matter. Attorney makes no such promises or guarantees. Attorney's comments about the outcome of the matter are expressions of opinion only. Any estimate of fees given by Attorney shall not be a guarantee. Actual fees may vary from estimates given.

This agreement contains the entire agreement between the parties. No other agreement, statement, or promise made on or before the effective date of this agreement, will be binding on the parties and it may be modified by agreement of the parties by an instrument in writing signed by both of them, or oral agreement, only to the extent that the parties carry it out.

If any provision of this agreement is held, in whole or in part, to be held unenforceable for any reason, the remainder of that provision and of the entire agreement will be severable, and remain in effect.

This agreement will take effect, and Attorney will have obligation to provide legal services when Client returns a signed copy of this agreement, and pays the initial deposit called for in the terms of the agreement. It shall govern all legal services performed by Attorney on behalf of Client commencing with the date the Attorney first performs services. The date of the beginning of this agreement is for reference only. Even if this agreement does not take effect, Client will be obligated to pay Attorney the reasonable value for any services Attorney may have performed for Client.

If a dispute arises between or among the parties hereto with regard to this agreement or any controversy arising from it or

continued

otherwise, the parties agree to mediate no less than three hours or until a settlement is reached, before submitting the matter to binding arbitration. The parties may agree on an arbitrator and if they cannot, any party may petition the court having jurisdiction over the matter to appoint such an arbitrator. The prevailing party in such disputes shall recover attorney fees.

The parties have read and understood for the foregoing terms, and agree to them as of the date Attorney first provided services. If more than one Client signs below, each agrees to be liable jointly and severally, for all obligations under this agreement. Clients will receive a fully executed duplicate of this agreement.

Dated _____, 20___, _____ (Client)

Address: _____

Telephone: _____

Dated: _____ (Attorney) by: _____

FEE STATEMENTS

Regardless of how you are compensated—contingency, retainer, or hourly—accurate time records must be kept. You may have to justify your reasonable fees on some occasions, particularly if you are terminated from the case and you have a lien. In other instances, you may be representing a client on a pro bono basis and the court awards attorney's fees. If you have not kept accurate time records, there is no way for the court to determine reasonable fees, except by guessing, and the guess may not be in your favor.

If you are representing a client on a retainer basis, the amount of the retainer is agreed in the fee agreement in advance. Your fee statement should show the amount remaining of the retainer plus the reduction for the current statement. When billing against a retainer, you should enclose an extra copy of the billing with a return envelope and a space on the copy for the client to initial next to the word "Approved." Because the retainer is in your client's trust account, you cannot reduce that amount without the authorization of the client, if you are using good accounting standards.

If you are billing on an hourly basis and the client is to pay the amount on the statement, this kind of authorization may be used, but is not necessary. The difference is the client sends you a check to pay for the amount on the bill rather than you taking it out of the trust account.

The method of billing should be discussed, determined, and agreed upon at the initial fee agreement session. The retainer in full should be taken immediately and deposited in the trust account. When the billing reaches a certain level against the retainer, the retainer should be replenished.

A suggested Billing Statement has been included on page 164 to give you the guidelines you will need for billing purposes.

Criminal Case Billing

If you decide to take a criminal case, you should determine what the fee is likely to be for the lifetime of the case, and collect that amount of money in advance as quickly as possible. In all cases, it is best to have the fee before you do the work, rather than take the case, do the work, and not get paid.

In a criminal case, if you do not take your fee in the beginning in full and the case goes to trial, you are subjected to one of two attitudes that are understandable but disastrous for you. First, if you win the case, the client says to you, "I was innocent anyway and did not need you." Second, if the case is lost, the client can say, "I was innocent and you bungled the case and I am not going to pay you."

Either way, you are caught in a dilemma of trying to get your fee from someone who is not motivated to do anything at all to help you get it. However, if the client is facing the prospect of the loss of freedom, they are quite motivated to help you get the fee up front so that you can get to work.

Provide Details

Regardless of how the billing takes place, accurate time records should be kept. The detail in the billing can be very significant for the client. For example, if you put on your timesheet "deposition of _____: 7 hours," the client will look at that and wonder why it took seven hours for one deposition. That same seven-hour time period can be billed in detail for the entire day to show that there was preparation time for the deposition, the first session of the deposition took this much time, the second session of the deposition took that much time, and the dictation of the deposition summary took place, each being a separate entry.

In such a situation, you may have lunch with cocounsel or with opposition counsel, and you may have discussed future deposition planning, or you may even have discussed settlement. If you just put down the seven hours, these important functions are lost. If you entered them in detail, the client is educated as to the detailed work you have done, and you may discover that the seven-hour day actually totals significantly more time. This kind of explanatory billing draws fewer criticisms from the client, and fewer requests for fee reduction. The function itself is related to the case, and has a rational time-related charge attributed to it. When the client is reviewing the bills, everything seems in order, makes sense, and it is, in fact, true.

Many people naturally have an aversion to paying legal fees. A well-drafted billing statement is not just a means of collecting your fees, but is also a very important opportunity to market yourself, your firm, and your staff because of the explanatory nature of the billing. The accurate description explaining the charges on a statement can be as important a marketing tool as taking a client for a round of golf or a fishing trip. Your client has an opportunity to see exactly what you are doing, and is more likely to give you more business.

A fee statement should also contain costs that are chargeable to the client, such as photocopying, postage, telephone and facsimile costs, parking, filing fees, messages, and other such costs.

Limitations

Many jurisdictions have fee limitations as to how much may be charged per hour for certain work, or how much may be charged in a contingency fee case. For example, certain probate courts have limits on the hourly fees that can be charged, and even have limitations on extraordinary fees. In representing minors for a personal injury matter, there may be restrictions on how much may be charged as a contingency fee. All of these special limitations should be noted not only in the fee agreement itself, but where applicable, should be noted on the fee statement—particularly the final one.

Be careful to research your jurisdictional limitations on fees before the fee agreement meeting and negotiation. If you need a subsequent meeting to discuss fees because you want to do more research, that is better than signing a fee agreement without knowing the limitations you are facing, and thus getting into an embroilment with your client when the case has been concluded.

When the fees are to be determined by a court or some other tribunal, there are some factors that are generally taken into consideration to determine what is a reasonable fee. These factors include:

- the experience and ability of the attorney performing the services;
- the time and effort expended;
- the uniqueness and difficulty of the issues involved;
- the skill required to perform the services;
- the amount recovered in the performing of services;
- the closeness and the links of the attorney/client relationship;
- the actual time spent on the performance of services;

- the charges for paralegal time;
- charges for travel, telephone calls, and other internal costs may be overhead and included in the fee rather than treated as extra costs; and,
- it is important that you examine the court rules or governing case law, or statutes dealing with matters such as probate, trusts, minors' cases and others that have the potential for special fee considerations.

FLAT FEES

Occasionally, you will have a client who wants to negotiate a flat fee. This is an old method of charging fees that was supplanted almost entirely by hourly fees, until recently. Clients who have a high volume of business with a relatively easily predictable expenditure of time like the flat fee because they can pay the fee, and then forget about dealing with the lawyers and their fees. Sometimes the flat fee is paid in installments or increments. Regardless of how it is paid, it is a motivation for the lawyer to conclude the matter as quickly as possible. Expenditure of time is less and the profit is higher, because overhead is being incurred all the time and the less overhead attributable to a particular file means more profit for the firm.

If a client wants you to negotiate a flat fee for certain services, you still must keep in mind the time that would be needed to perform the services and convert them into hours or estimated hours in order to determine if the flat fee is fair. One of the best ways to determine this when you are beginning a law firm is to talk to other lawyers who are handling similar cases and get their estimates as to how much time will be spent in discovery, research, and trial times. Frequently, the flat fee cases are repetitious, they have little research involved, and most of the cases settle, so that you are not involved in lengthy trials. A reasonable estimate of time required can be made for the client and the flat fee is fair to all. Remember, you must keep time sheets because the court just might award *reasonable attorney's fees*.

BILLABLE TIME

Self-discipline is the most important component of keeping track of billable time. Promptly recording every chargeable time you spend on your client's case must become a habit. It may be an effective exercise for you to keep track of every significant time, whether it is billable or not. This not only keeps you in the habit of billing for time, but may also give you a better understanding of how you are expending your working days.

You may accumulate time for mandatory continuing legal education, such as attending workshops, seminars, and meetings with appropriate keynote speakers. This habit will be beneficial to you when you are collecting the time to prepare a billing statement for your client. If you attend an educational seminar on a subject that benefits certain files in your office and write a significantly beneficial memorandum to the file about what you have learned at that meeting or seminar, it could form the basis for a reasonable charge of time for that file. If you are not keeping accurate time, you may never know that you spent that time creating value for your client's file, and that you should be compensated for it.

Remember, you can always give your client the benefit of the doubt and reduce the time charged to certain services, but it is difficult to increase them if you do not record the time when it is expended. You should record each entry of time that you spend on a client's file and each expense incurred on behalf of your client's file. Record every phone call, and record time and mileage from the beginning of your travel on behalf of your client to the destination and return.

It is tempting to temper the amount of time recorded for a particular event, based upon the success or failure of that event. It is wiser to wait until the billing statement is being prepared to adjust the billing for the success or failure you may have in the case. It is understandable that you would want to give the client the benefit of the doubt if the case is long. It is equally understandable that if you are successful, to give yourself the benefit of the doubt in estimating the time spent on a certain matter in the case when the outcome was unclear. If you have precisely recorded the time, there would be no need to adjust it.

Time Sheets

The physical process of preparing billing systems is not complicated. Rather than create your own system, it is much more practical to use a system that is produced commercially. There are both paper and electronic billing systems available and they can be found in legal bookstores, supply houses, journals, and websites devoted to legal publications.

You should use a time-keeping system that is most satisfying to you. Some have complicated duplications, and you may not need all of the details contained in a particular system. It is sufficient to have the case number, name, client name, date, description space, and time space.

Ideally, a time sheet is prepared for each day. The space is filled in for every billable activity for that day, so you can work on multiple files in one day and the time will be allotted to each respective file in the billing statement.

If you use an electronic system, there is always the danger that data will be deleted. As in other electronic applications for vital data, your billing records should be stored in a redundant system or printed to make a permanent record.

CONTINGENCY FEES

This kind of agreement with the client is compensation based upon the contingency that the client will make a recovery. The attorney's fee is a percentage of that, which is usually negotiated or based upon the current custom for that particular kind of case involved in the representation. The contingency fee case is the source of a great deal of income, and can be quite lucrative.

Conversely, if the client does not prevail, the attorney receives nothing by way of a fee. The client may be saddled with costs that are recoverable in the litigation, and the client may be personally liable for these. In some fee agreements, the costs are to be absorbed by the attorney. The percentage of the contingency fee usually reflects this added responsibility for the attorney.

Generally speaking, the lawyer in a contingency case advances costs for such things as expert witnesses, investigators, demonstrative evidence, and other services that are necessary to prosecute the case. If there is no recovery by the client, the attorney absorbs these costs and fees, even if the contingency fee agreement may state otherwise. An attorney can lose a great deal of money in contingency fee case losses.

Time sheets are just as important in a contingency fee case as they are where time records are expected. When the attorney for the client in a contingency case is terminated by the client, by death, or by any other means, the contingency fee will no longer be applicable in all likelihood. The only recovery by the attorney's estate or successor's interest is reasonable attorney's fees in almost all jurisdictions.

When the attorney is terminated, a lien can be placed on the case, and when the judgment or verdict is in favor of the client, the lien can be enforced by the trial court. In order to justify the amounts claimed in the lien, time records are the best way to show the amount of work and effort that has gone into the case, in addition to costs that the client may have to pay, such as the filing fee. Even in contingency fee cases, keeping time records help you to maintain quality control and better evaluation of the work done on a case.

In a contingency case, you have a technical and ethical responsibility. All settlement negotiations must be communicated to the client. The client alone must decide to settle. If asked, you may express an opinion, but never coerce or direct your client.

A suggested Billing Statement is included on page 164 to give you some basic ideas as to what you should include in your statement. A Client Satisfaction Response Form is on page 165, because you may want to send that out periodically to your client. It is difficult when clients are critical, but it is more difficult when they are critical and you do not know it. Sometimes the only way you know about client dissatisfaction is when they file a lawsuit against you or they simply do not engage your services any longer. Remember, billing is also client relations development and marketing.

Billing Statement

Law Offices of _____

Date: _____

Client's Address: _____

_____

Statement for Legal Services

_____, 20____ through _____, 20____

Subject Re: _____ vs. _____.

Our File No.: _____

Responsible Attorney: _____

Date:	Description of services	Hourly Time	Hourly Fee	Total Fees

Date:	Copying	Telephone/ Fax	Postage	Court Charges	

Services Rendered:

Total Fees & Charges: _____

Due and payable upon receipt.

Please make your check payable to _____.

[A reduction in retainer must be authorized]

Retainer reduction hereby authorized: _____

Client Satisfaction Response Form

_____ [Firm name] appreciates the opportunity to provide you with legal services. We are always trying to improve our client care and would be very grateful if you would take a moment to answer the questions below and return this form in the postage-paid envelope provided.

1. Have our front office personnel been friendly and helpful? ☐Yes ☐No

2. Have your calls and office visits been handled courteously? ☐Yes ☐No

3. Have other office personnel—secretaries, clerks, accounting staff, etc.—treated you with respect? ☐Yes ☐No

4. Were your telephone calls returned promptly? ☐Yes ☐No

5. Were the lawyers attentive and prepared in your case? ☐Yes ☐No

6. Were the details of your case or concern explained to you clearly? ☐Yes ☐No

7. Were you updated regularly regarding the progress of your case? ☐Yes ☐No

8. Did a client referred you to our firm? ☐Yes ☐No

9. Would you refer potential clients to our firm? ☐Yes ☐No

10. Would you like to receive additional information from our firm, such as a short newsletter with current updates? ☐Yes ☐No

ALTERNATIVE DISPUTE RESOLUTION

Since the 1980s, people involved in businesses and professions have increasingly required in their contracts the use of arbitration and mediation to resolve disputes arising out of those contracts. The use of arbitration gives the parties the advantage of having their disputes resolved in a manner which is fast, fair, and final. Mediation adds flexibility to the dispute resolution process.

The trial format is the most expensive of all of the dispute resolution formats, and the cost of litigation is a very important factor in the motivation of people to settle cases before they go to trial. The expense of a trial is probably the number one reason why 95% of all cases settle before a trial. There are certain cases, however, that must go to trial, and the risks and expense cannot be avoided.

Because of these risks, you can now understand why it is important to include mediation and arbitration clauses in your retainer contracts. Many of these engagement contracts require a minimum time for mediation, and if it is unsuccessful, the matter goes to arbitration. The appellate courts have held repeatedly that contracts requiring alternative dispute resolution (ADR) are valid.

One of the risks involved in litigation is the situation where you are seeking your professional fees. Such a lawsuit inevitably draws a cross claim for professional liability or malpractice. It is much more to your advantage to have these disputes resolved outside of the trial format. Thus, the ADR requirements in your contracts become even more important to the success of your practice.

chapter thirteen:
Marketing Your Firm

The practice of law cannot exist in any form without clients. While some lawyers optimistically sign a lease for an office space, invest thousands of dollars in computers and office equipment, hire a secretary or receptionist, and then wait for clients to come through the door. Such an approach seldom succeeds. You must have clients before you open your law firm.

To get clients, you need to promote your business. *Marketing* is a catchall word that includes all forms of advertising, public relations, direct mail, printed and online materials, and professional and community networking. Marketing your business is an essential component of your business plan and your budget, and you should think of it as a vital part of building your career. While your marketing budget should not be calculated strictly as a percentage of gross revenues, established businesses typically spend 2–5% of gross profits on marketing, while new businesses may spend 10–15% of gross for the first couple of years.

Good marketing requires time and talent. While you may have terrific networking skills, you should seek professional help for some of the more specialized aspects of marketing, such as graphic design and public relations. It is not realistic to expect that you or your secretary—who has more pressing responsibilities and specialized skills—will be able to manage the various aspects of your marketing program. An advertising agency can handle all of your promotions—from Yellow Page listings to brochures, websites, and public appearances—but their fees may exceed your budget. Freelance writers, graphic designers, and marketing consultants may be able to assist you more efficiently. Ask your colleagues and local bar association for referrals to individuals and firms with experience in marketing for lawyers. As you are developing the marketing section of your business plan, interview graphic designers, advertising firms, and public relations specialists and ask for proposals.

For the first three-quarters of the 20ᵗʰ century, lawyers were prohibited from advertising their services. This was to protect the public from false and misleading claims, called *puffery*, and legal jargon that could be misconstrued. In 1977, the United States Supreme Court modified that prohibition in *Bates v. State Bar of Arizona*, ruling that lawyers could advertise certain information in newspapers, in magazines, in the Yellow Pages, on billboards, and on radio and television, as long as those ads did not contain false or misleading information.

The American Bar Association's Center for Professional Responsibility defines the standards for marketing and posts their Model Rules of Professional Conduct, available on the ABA website. Rule 7.1, *Communications Concerning a Lawyer's Services*, states, "A lawyer shall not make a false or misleading communication about the lawyer or the lawyer's services. A communication is false or misleading if it contains a material misrepresentation of fact or law, or omits a fact necessary to make the statement considered as a whole not materially misleading."

Rule 7.2, *Advertising*, states, "…a lawyer may advertise services through written, recorded or electronic communication, including public media" and goes on to define the standards that govern referrals within the industry. Rule 7.5, *Firm Names and Letterheads*, explains the standards of promotion that apply to trade names, multiple-jurisdiction law firms, lawyers holding a public office, and partnerships.

All of these rules must be considered carefully as you prepare your marketing materials. Also, be sure to consult your state bar association for any local rulings that may apply.

FIRST THINGS FIRST

As soon as you have decided upon your firm's name, address, and other contact information, meet with your graphic designer to discuss the design of your business cards and letterhead. These essential tools will be necessary in virtually every aspect of your professional life, so the sooner they are printed and in your hands, the better.

Your printed materials impart an important message about your firm. The conventions of design for lawyers' cards and letterheads are fairly conservative. Heavy, smooth paper stock suggests dignity, sophistication, and success, and if you are trying to appeal to affluent individuals or corporations, it is well worth the additional cost. Colored inks, glossy papers, and photographs are sometimes used on business cards by personal injury lawyers, but even they might want to have a *toned-down* version to exchange with professional colleagues.

Always ask your designer or printer for a final proof, and read it over carefully. Read every single word and number. Your business card is useless if your name is misspelled or your phone number or email address is one number or character off. Do not assume that because the address is correct on your business cards, it is also correct on your letterhead and envelopes. Take the time to proofread. If you do not, and there is a typo, you will have to bear the cost and delays of reprinting your materials.

Your initial marketing materials should also include a formal announcement of the opening of your firm. This is typically a *panel* card—a single pane without folds—and matching envelope. Again, use the best quality paper you can afford, ideally, very similar to your business cards. This is likely to be your first official piece of marketing for your firm, and it should reach the broadest possible audience—your contacts from law school, lawyers, businesspeople in your community, family members, friends—in short, anyone who knows you or might be able to send business your way.

BUILDING A BASE

Marketing has two phases—getting clients and keeping them. The former includes two audiences—the people or businesses that will be using your services directly and the people or businesses that will be able to refer clients to you. For example, if you practice personal injury law, your primary audience is the general public, but once you are established in the community, you may find that a lot of your business is coming from insurance companies, doctors, and other lawyers. Your marketing should target both audiences.

If you do not have an established base of clients, how do you build one? One of the basic means of making contact with potential clients is to join civic or charitable organizations and become active. This may include chambers of commerce, networking groups, religious organizations, charities, and even athletic clubs. There is almost no networking value in such groups if you do not participate, so simply paying the dues to get on a membership list is a very expensive and ineffective form of marketing. Attend meeting and events. Talk with people. Hand out business cards. Get interested in other people's lives, and before long, they will take an interest in yours.

Offering your services as a speaker or panelist is a very good way of making yourself known as a lawyer and an expert in your field. For example, your jurisdiction may have recently enacted legislation or ordinances that govern specific subjects, such as curfews for minors. There may be new legislation or significant court rulings involving civil liabilities, personal injury, or limitations on punitive damages. Such subjects may become the focus of interest to business or community groups.

Identify current issues that are of interest to your potential clients. If you practice real estate law, you might plan a talk on the ten most common legal mistakes people make when they buy real estate. If you are an estate-planning attorney, your subject might be "What is probate?"

You are competing with television and everything else that your audience could be doing instead of listening to you, so picking a good topic—and then delivering a great presentation—is your challenge. You have to provide information of value to your audience so they feel it was worth the sacrifice—and they will get the subtle message that you are someone who delivers on a promise.

It is up to you to make your presentation—whatever the subject matter—as thought-provoking as possible. Prepare as thoroughly as you can. Rehearse your talk, add humor and visual aids, and start and end on time. Consider putting together a handout that recaps the most important points of your presentation. Have your handout printed on your letterhead and attach a business card to it. Carry plenty of additional business cards—you should be handing out at least ten a day as you are setting up your practice—and your brochure, if you happen to have one.

In preparing, you can also take a page from presidential candidates, who drill themselves on every possible question that could be asked of them in a public forum. If you take the time to imagine the worst-case scenario and the most devastating questions, and prepare yourself with answers, your public presentations will be a breeze.

If you begin your firm by buying an existing practice, you have a built-in base not only for clients, but a network upon which to build. The firm's clients may decide to stay with you or they may decide to move on to other counsel. It is your job to hold the practice together, maintain the client base, and expand on it. You should consider having a reception where the outgoing or retiring lawyer introduces you, the incoming lawyer, to the clients, thereby easing the transition.

Taking on a celebrated case either at a reduced fee or on a pro bono basis can demonstrate to the community how talented you are as an attorney, and that you are someone to be trusted because you have volunteered yourself so graciously. Media coverage will almost certainly make the phone ring.

Your community may also offer other opportunities for pro bono work, such as volunteer lawyers for the arts. You may also wish to join a panel of lawyers to be appointed by the court to represent indigent criminal defendants. Such work expands your professional network, provides excellent opportunities for mentoring, and helps to cement your reputation as a pillar of the community.

You can also expand your practice with work on a contract basis. This is a way for you to become known in the legal community. You can make court appearances, deposition appearances, and do other contract legal work for firms that want to augment or increase their services by engaging independent lawyers. Additionally, referrals to smaller cases will be available to you if the firms know that you are willing to take on smaller matters, such as collections, unlawful detainers, workers' compensation, and other concerns that larger firms are unwilling to accept.

You may also want to offer free initial consultations to potential clients if providing it meets the standards of your local bar association. If you are new in the community, this opens the door and helps to build awareness of your services.

If you have a well-defined area of expertise and reasonable writing skills, you may wish to write articles for consumer publications. For example, if you are an expert in entertainment law, you could write an article titled "The Ten Most

Important Clauses in Your Recording Contract" for a musicians' magazine. You would probably not be paid for the article, but it would reach your target audience, and your name and contact information would appear as part of your credit.

ADVERTISING

Promoting yourself in print and electronic media may be essential or have limited value, depending upon the nature of your practice. At a minimum, you may want to list yourself in the Yellow Pages or publications such as the *Martindale-Hubbell Law Directory*.

Advertising is, in general, costly, short-lived, and only works through repetition. The cost per ad decreases if you contract for multiple ads. Advertising must be targeted carefully to a specific audience. For example, if you practice corporate or real estate law and your community publishes a business journal, it may be worthwhile to purchase a contract for six months or a year's worth of advertising. Billboard and radio advertising are often used by personal injury lawyers. These ads successfully reach a large part of their potential client base—people in cars.

Some lawyers also use direct mail as a way of reaching potential clients. Once you define your audience, mailing lists can be purchased that are targeted to that group.

Again, depending upon your practice, you may wish to produce a company brochure, though a website may be a better investment for a young firm. Quality brochures are costly to produce and difficult to update. In general, a brochure, whether paper or electronic, should outline your firm's philosophy, areas of specialty, and credentials. Unlike ads, which reach out to your audience, brochures and websites are more passive marketing. They are complementary to all of the other marketing you do and should not be relied upon as your sole means of promotion. Work with a professional designer to create an image that will appeal to your clients. Keep text simple, direct, short, and easy to read. And, of course, proofread, proofread, proofread.

KEEPING CLIENTS

Once you have clients—and referral sources—you need to keep them. All the marketing in the world will not make up for bad service, so your first concern should be to deliver the best professional service you possibly can.

Returning phone calls is a critical component of your marketing program. If you fail to return phone calls, answer letters, or reply to emails, you are undermining everything else you do to promote your business.

Get in the habit of saying "thank you." When you get a referral, whether it comes from another lawyer, a family member, a friend, or someone else, take the time immediately to express your appreciation. A handwritten thank you note is the most gracious way to do this, but a phone call or email will suffice. Do not wait to see if the referral turns into a client. Express your appreciation for the thought. If it turns out that the referral is a lucrative case, further thanks are in order.

Networking with clients and colleagues also helps to keep your business alive. Plan to have lunch at least once a week with a client or colleague you do not see very often. These lunches do not need to have an agenda. They merely keep the lines of communication open and keep you fresh in the minds of your important contacts.

Finally, remember that marketing is an investment. The money you put into your firm today will probably not yield immediate results. However, if approached thoughtfully, consistently, and within the parameters of professional standards, your marketing will help you to develop a strong, successful image that will serve your law practice for years to come.

chapter fourteen:
Effective Correspondence

Quite often, the correspondence you receive from opposing counsel can be oppressive, intimidating, and daunting. Your correspondence should be professional, fair, and courteous. You should develop a habit of drafting correspondence that sends the message that you want, but worded in a professional manner.

The following are some general guidelines for your professional correspondence.

- Begin each paragraph with positive words, such as "Thank you," "Fortunately," "Hopefully," "Happily," and "Please."
- Do not begin paragraphs with the words "I," "We," "Our," "Unfortunately," "Regrettably," or any other word that has a negative or egotistical connotation.
- Use short paragraphs that contain no more than three sentences.
- Use long paragraphs only to bury bad news, and put the bad news in the middle of the paragraph.
- Begin and end a letter with an upbeat or positive sentence, if possible.

- Show that a copy of the letter is sent to someone else who is relevant to the correspondence. This underscores accountability in that someone else will be reading the letter.

Sample letters are provided on the following pages as suggestions for use with your own modifications, as appropriate to your situation. Although these are examples, the above guidelines are applicable to all business correspondence and particularly to clients.

SUGGESTED CORRESPONDENCE

Letter Regarding Mediation

[Firm Letterhead]

[Date]

[Addressee]

Re: _____ vs. _____

Our File No.: _____

Our Client: _____

Dear _____:

Thank you for responding to my letter of _____, 20___. I am glad that you agree with me that mediation is the way we should try to resolve this case.

Please find attached a list of suggested mediators, as well as available dates within the next six weeks for my client and for me.

You may call me at any time to discuss the information on the attached lists, and we can formalize an agreement as to the mediator and the appropriate dates.

Sincerely,

_____

Letter Dealing with Difficult Attorney

[Firm Letterhead]

[Date]

[Addressee]

Re: _____ vs. _____

Our File No.: _____

Our Client: _____

Dear _____:

Your request for an extension of time for your client's deposition, now set for _____, was conveyed to me by my secretary.

You will recall several months ago I requested an extension of time for my client's deposition, and you declined to grant me a continuance. My client had to attend a family funeral, and I was required to make an ex parte appearance before the court to obtain an extension for the deposition. The appearance cost my client considerably.

Hopefully, you will find a replacement for your secretary who quit suddenly, [or whatever the excuse] and I wish you well.

Please understand that my calendar is quite crowded and I have to decline your request for such an extension.

Sincerely,

_____

Letter Sending Bad News to the Client

[Firm Letterhead]

[Date]

[Addressee]

Re: _____ vs. _____

Our File No.: _____

Our Client: _____

Dear _____:

Fortunately, the court granted our request to shorten time so that our Motion to Dismiss could be made at the same time as the Trial Setting Conference. We now have a Trial date set for _____.

The court heard the Motion and spent quite a bit of time listening to the Arguments on both sides.

The court complimented our firm for the high quality of our brief and followed our argument intently. The court found that a question of fact remained, and denied our motion and felt that fifteen hundred dollars in sanctions should be paid to the other side and, of course, our firm will take care of that. These things are a matter of a judgment call, and we tried our best to get the matter concluded.

Thank you for your cooperation in this difficult case. All of us here look forward to working with you in prevailing at trial.

Sincerely,

_____

Letter Terminating the Client Relationship

[Firm Letterhead]

[Date]

[Addressee]

Re: _____ vs. _____

Our File No.: _____

Our Client: _____

Dear _____:

This confirms our recent telephone conversation (or correspondence) regarding our outstanding fees of _____.

It is axiomatic that legal services must be paid before an attorney can proceed further in representing a client.

Our firm (or I) has (have) represented you thus far in the above matter and the fees in question have been earned.

You have been sent (the number) of statements and letters seeking payment. Now we cannot proceed any further. We will make arrangements to have a Substitution of Attorney sent to you if you do not respond within five working days from the above date.

Please let us know if you have followed our previous advice and obtained new counsel.

Sincerely,

_____

Notice of Settlement Offer

[Firm Letterhead]

[Date]

[Addressee]

Re: _____ vs. _____

    Date of Incident _____

Dear _____:

Thank you for discussing this matter with me on the telephone, on _____ (date). This confirms that we discussed the settlement offer made by the opposition in the amount of $_____.

Please contact me if you wish to discuss the matter in addition to what we have already covered in our conversation, as I am prepared today to convey to them the results of your decision.

Sincerely,

_____

Settlement Fund Distribution Letter

[Firm Letterhead]

[Date]

[Addressee]

Re: _____ vs. _____

    Date of Accident _____

Dear _____:

You will be pleased to know that after our conversation on _____[date], we received an offer from the opposition in full settlement of the above matter in the amount of $_____. This settlement amount would be distributed as set out below, in accordance with our agreement at the outset of this case:

Gross amount . . . . $_____
Less expense . . . . $_____
Medical reports. . . . . $_____
Filing fees . . . . $_____
Out of pocket costs . . . . $_____
Total expenses . . . . $_____
Balance . . . . $_____
Our fee (as agreed) . . . . $_____
Balance . . . . $_____
Medical liens/expenses. . . . . $_____
Net to you . . . . $_____

Please sign and date the enclosed copy of this letter and return it to me in the envelope provided, if the above is acceptable and agreeable to you.

If you have any questions, or wish to discuss any aspect of the contents of this letter, please call me immediately. If you have any tax questions, please contact your tax advisor.

Sincerely,

_____[Attorney]

I have read and understand and agree to the above.

Date:_____, 20_____

_____[Client]

Section Three:
Personal Considerations

chapter fifteen:
Ethics

When a person acts for and controls the property and resources for another, as well as the personal affairs and even the livelihood of others, it becomes absolutely necessary that stringent ethical standards be required. Traditionally, the legal profession has established the highest ethical duties of the attorney toward the client. That is why the attorney/client privilege is held in such sacred status. A client must be able to reveal everything to the attorney in order to obtain the best legal advice. This advice may lead to a guilty plea to a crime, but that may be the best legal advice that the client could hope for under the circumstances. Law practioners are expected, therefore, to be righteous, virtuous, and even noble.

Although this is not a book devoted solely to ethics in the practice of law, it is important when beginning your law firm that you learn some of the ethical considerations expected of you as the person in charge and responsible for the conduct of your firm. That includes overseeing the conduct of several people. It is your duty to maintain reasonable vigilance over those who work for you to maintain the high ethical standards expected in the legal profession.

If you find attorneys, paralegals, or staff cutting corners or doing things that are even slightly unethical, the best thing for you and your firm to do is to give them a warning. If they fail to head the warning, tell them that they will be very happy working some place else. If the conduct is egregious enough, they do not deserve a warning and definitely should be invited to find another place of employment.

You must not lose sight of the fact that the practice of law must also be run as a business. A lawyer who has a reputation as an unethical practitioner will eventually have few, if any, clients, and will turn to some other endeavor to make a living.

It is difficult to be an ethical lawyer. It is stressful, it is time-consuming, and it provides many temptations for dishonesty. But the overwhelming majority of lawyers succeed and thrive ethically.

ETHICAL RULES

The American Bar Association provides the Model Rules of Professional Conduct; the respective state jurisdictions also have rules of conduct. Because the ABA rules are not binding on any of the states (unless the model rule has been adopted by those states), the rules of the bar to which you belong are governing, and the bar exam touches only the tip of the iceberg with respect to ethics. The thing that is probably best to remember is that if someone's conduct, including yours, raises the slightest doubt in your mind as to whether or not it is ethical, then it is probably unethical.

If the question is close enough that you might want to have a discussion or seek an outside opinion, then look to your bar association for guidance. Most have an ethics hotline connection, or some other means of obtaining advice or counseling. As is the case in many situations, the rules cannot be written to cover every situation. Consequently, broad and general ethical rules must be applied to the specific situation at hand.

A good suggestion for someone beginning a practice of law is to read the discipline reports contained in bar association publications and legal newspapers, as well as other sources for such information about the law and its specific function. It will take only a short time of examining these reports to learn how lawyers can get into professional trouble or disbarred for doing things that would not be quite so important in other circumstances or professions.

There are certain things that are specifically unethical. One of them is threatening criminal action against anyone in order to coerce the settlement or resolution of a civil claim. This is true in some jurisdictions even when no civil action is pending. Just the threat of criminal action is sufficient to bring the appropriate discipline upon the offender.

ETHICS AND PERSONNEL

Another area where ethical considerations can be troublesome is in the invidious discrimination against individuals in employment, engagement for services, or in other aspects of the practice of law. This discrimination is defined by most jurisdictions as discrimination based upon race, gender, national origin, sexual orientation, religion, age, or disability. For this reason, it is wise to keep all applications for employment and résumés of people who are interviewed for employment for two years in order to have your notes available as to the reason why someone was not hired.

The same standards can, of course, apply to your treatment of office clerks, paralegals, staff, and attorneys employed by you. Violations of these standards are governed by Title VII of the *Civil Rights Act of 1964*.

In selecting the people you interview for positions, remember that there are certain areas that you are ethically prevented from exploring, such as a person's age, marital status, ethnicity, or anything else that borders on such subject matter. Conversely, there are laws prohibiting you from hiring people in the country illegally, so it becomes a delicate balance as to how you gather necessary information without also violating someone's civil rights. Read through the hiring rules found in any good book on the subject.

Unauthorized Practice of Law

Paralegals, law clerks, and other staff may be of great assistance to you, and can perform many tasks within the practice of law under your supervision. This frees your time for court appearances, depositions, and other things that they cannot do. It is very tempting for lawyers to send paralegals to settlement conferences and other legal appearances. However, the practice is fraught with danger, both for the paralegal for practicing law without a license, and the attorney who is aiding and abetting the unlawful practice of law, both of which can be at least misdemeanors. Most jurisdictions are very careful and concerned about attorneys aiding and abetting anyone else in violation of professional rules of conduct, especially the practice of law without a license.

You should always remember that the attorneys and staff who work under your supervision are your responsibility as far as ethics are concerned. This is particularly true if a lawyer under a bar association discipline is working for you. These lawyers are required to not do anything that is the practice of law, and it is easy for them to slip into what lawyers do, particularly since they have slipped at least once before. Be very careful in hiring and having these people working for you on legal matters.

ATTORNEY RELATIONS WITH THE PUBLIC

An attorney may not engage in any conduct that deceives or misleads a court or any judicial officers. Usually, the attorney's duty is much broader than that, and the attorney may not engage in deception of any party under any circumstance. This is one of the most common misconceptions the public has about attorneys: that they are deceitful, sly, and will use any technicality whatsoever to prevail, no matter how inequitable it may be. This is the kind of behavior that attorneys should avoid, particularly as you are beginning your law firm. You do not want to gain the reputation of being that kind of practitioner.

Attorneys have a duty to report to their bar association any breaches of fiduciary duty, civil judgments, criminal convictions, or any other incidents that may reflect on the ethical standards of an attorney. In some jurisdictions, non-discovery sanctions exceeding $1,000 must be reported to the state bar. Attorneys have been disciplined for not reporting such sanctions. If the matters accumulate, the discipline could be severe and made public, which would seriously injure the attorney's reputation.

The most damaging charges an attorney can face are those involving acts of *moral turpitude*. The bar must be notified by prosecuting attorneys of any actions against an attorney involving a felony or misdemeanor. The reason for this is so that the determination of acts of moral turpitude can be made, and the trial courts may remind the prosecuting attorney of such an obligation.

The term *moral turpitude* is used as a term of art in determining whether or not an attorney should be disciplined severely. *Turpitude* is defined as conduct that is base, vile, or depraved. Conduct that is unconnected with the practice of law, but is found to be of moral turpitude, can result in discipline.

The American Bar Association Model Rule 8.3 requires an attorney to report ethical violations of other attorneys. That may not be a requirement of other local jurisdictions, but it seems to fit as a pattern that may be a trend. For example, the *Sarbanes-Oxley Act* provides that an attorney may have a duty to inform the Securities and Exchange Commission of corporate illegalities that they may have learned about in their employment. This raises attorney/client privilege problems.

Jurors

It is a good rule to follow—without any exceptions—that where you are involved in a case with jurors, jurors make minimal contact with you. Although the jurors are instructed that they are not to discuss the case with anyone prior to deliberation, some of them cannot resist the temptation to strike up a conversation with a lawyer, and run a few things past the lawyer to get an opinion. This is a clear violation of the juror's oath, and if the lawyer responds in any way other than an objection, it violates the lawyer's ethical standards in dealing with the juror. The juror is obviously going outside the evidence of the case and outside the instructions of the court to arrive at a verdict.

chapter sixteen:
Good
Attorney/Client Relations

In addition to maintaining loyalty to your clients and avoiding conflicts of interest, the day-to-day relationship with clients in the practice of law is the most important way in which to further your business. This also lessens complaints and malpractice lawsuits by your clients. Studies have shown that clients want their lawyers to show dedication to them and to communicate with them. They want these two things even more than they want their attorneys to be competent.

Clients are like customers in any other business. They want, in addition to those two things, quality legal services, reasonable fees, open communication, and the feeling that you are taking good care of them.

Complaints to a state bar are increasing as society's attitudes change toward attorneys. As people are increasingly more willing to sue their attorneys, and jurors are expressing their dissatisfaction with lawyers' conduct, these lawsuits are not expected to go down in number in the near future. The majority of complaints against attorneys come from clients who have cases involving family law, workers' compensation, and personal injury. The number one complaint is that the attorney did not return telephone calls. *Failed to respond to written communications* does not fall not far behind. Answering the client's telephone calls is as important to your success as your legal abilities, in the client's view.

It cannot be repeated enough that the relationship between attorney and client is a unique and personal one. This applies to all relationships, whether it is family law, corporate law, litigation of any kind, or workers' compensation. Attorneys should always keep in mind that even though they may be representing a giant corporation in a matter, their contact with that corporation is through its human representatives and their feelings toward the attorney are the same as an individual client. They expect loyalty and trust. If a client begins to feel that the lawyer cannot be trusted, the relationship will be over rather quickly, and it is not, in any way, good for the attorney.

This kind of dissatisfaction can manifest itself in a malpractice claim. One of the most devastating feelings any lawyer can have is to be sued for malpractice. It is one of the most direct attacks on a lawyer's personal self-esteem. The chief complaint in malpractice cases is the lawyer's lack of competency in communication skills. Misunderstandings concerning attorney's fees are also claims that are the basis for many malpractice losses. Nearly half of the claims made against lawyers stem from simple failures in client relations.

This same problem exists in fee disputes for clients. The two most important things that trigger fee disputes are lack of communication by the attorney with the client and the absence of a written fee agreement. These two lapses are easily remedied. They are simple in nature. They do not require anyone to go to law school or anyone to pass the bar.

They require only that the lawyer be sensitive to the needs of the client, which are basic and sometimes not even related to the issues of the case.

Clients often just want to talk to the lawyer to be reassured. If there is no fee agreement, the misunderstandings and lack of trust that clients want to avoid become unavoidable. Regardless of how long your relationships with a client, it is imperative that a written fee agreement be entered into before you begin working on any matter. Once the relationship with a client turns bad, it may be too late to save the client for your firm. Therefore, the best course of action is to establish a good relationship before things get out of hand.

FIRST IMPRESSIONS

Obviously, if you are beginning a law firm, you want to exercise the first opportunity to make a good impression. You want to furnish good legal services for your client, and you want to give good customer service. All of these motivations are to be expected.

Carrying those good intentions out in practice is the test of a successful practice. If you are able to do that, you will take your beginning practice into the future with healthy growth and the feeling of personal satisfaction that you are helping your clients, serving the public, and making a good living while doing so.

Meet with your clients at a place where you can feel comfortable with them. If this place is in your office, it should be in surroundings that are not noisy, cluttered, or distracting. Some lawyers meet with their clients in a quiet conference room, adorned with law books, which creates an atmosphere of trust and strength.

You may want to meet your client at a fine restaurant or a club, where the atmosphere is also one of trust and graciousness. The privacy that clients may need for some matters determines where you will hold your meetings.

In most of the places mentioned, there are no phones, and you can be reached only for emergencies. If you must carry your cell phone with you, explain to your client that you are waiting for a call, and put your phone on a silent alarm or vibrate. This will ensure that you will not attract others' attention—but you can answer your phone. If your client thinks that you are willing to interrupt the meeting to serve another client in cases of emergency, you will do the same to meet his or her needs in a time of crisis.

When you want to introduce your attorneys, paralegals, and staff to your client, be as gracious as you would when you introduce two friends. The gesture gives a clear but unstated indication to the client that you trust the people you are introducing the client to, and the client can trust them as well. This helps establish a personal relationship, so that when a client calls the office and speaks to staff, he or she can call the staff by name. If you are out of the office and another attorney has to assist the client, there is no problem because the client knows the attorney and the client's trust in the office in general is attributable to the attorney as well.

TERMINATING A CLIENT

Terminating a relationship with a client is always a situation involving mixed emotions. If the matter has been handled successfully and the client no longer needs your services, it is a happy departure, and everyone leaves satisfied. If the contrary is true, the client and you may both have difficulties in parting.

For whatever reason the termination occurs, all files belonging to the client should be offered to be returned to the client, with a copy retained for your records. Properties and things held for the client should be offered to be returned. Any unused portions of retainers, trust fund, or any money due to the client for any reason should be returned immediately.

If the client demands his or her file, holding it until fees are paid is a violation of the professional ethics that you must follow. You should make a copy of the entire file, return the file to the client, and make some other arrangement to obtain unpaid fees. Even the slightest suggestion of coercion by an attorney regarding a client is ill-advised.

After termination of a relationship, the question of how long the attorney should maintain the client's file arises. The attorney is responsible for a client's file that is destroyed prematurely, so it is wise to err on the side of caution. Some jurisdictions have file limitations on how long an attorney should maintain a file, but some do not. A good range is five to seven years.

The file belongs to the client. After the applicable appeal time or other time limitations have expired, you should give your clients the opportunity to have the file sent to them. Clients will quite often say that they want you to keep it. If that is the case, you must maintain it for them. The situation varies with the kind of case. If you have probate and trust files, and you have custody of original documents in your safe, that affects how long you must keep the file.

If there is a lengthy, involved business transaction with contracts and agreements that stretch out into the future many years, that will affect how long you keep the file. If the file is a personal injury file and the case has resolved by way of settlement or judgment, you may only want to keep the file for three years, at which time you offer it to your client. If your client in such a case was a minor, you probably want to keep the file for as long at it takes the minor to reach adulthood.

If your firm closes its doors, what do you do with file storage when there is no successor firm to take over? This is when professional private storage companies can be helpful. There are storage companies that will maintain such files in safe environments, and the cost is relatively low. Nevertheless, you should make every effort to have your client take the file, and you keep a copy for your records to protect yourself in case of malpractice in the future. If you cannot locate your client, you must make a reasonable effort to do so before you dispose of the file. You must show that you have exercised due diligence in your search.

If you purchase another attorney's practice to take it over or make it part of your own, you may then be responsible for maintaining the storage of that firm's files. Whoever is left with the firm has that responsibility, and it could be somewhat burdensome. All of these issues are to be ironed out by negotiation and agreement before the problem gets out of hand.

CLIENT COMMUNICATIONS

The most common complaint clients have with regard to their relationships with attorneys is the failure of the attorneys to communicate with the client. That not only includes the developments in the case or matters at hand, but also keeping in touch to answer any questions that the client may have. It is imperative that you answer all telephone calls and all correspondence. Certainly, a large percentage of malpractice suits can be avoided merely by responding to the client's phone calls and letters, even when bad news has to be delivered.

There is no excuse for the attorney's failure to keep the client informed of the current status of the matter that the attorney is handling. If clients fail to keep you aware of their whereabouts, it is your duty to expend more than reasonable efforts to try to locate your client. Not only is this a duty imposed upon you by your profession and its rules of conduct, but it is a practical matter as well. If your client disappears and this renders your work impossible to go forward, you want to have a clear track record of your attempts to make contact with the client. If the matter involves a court action, you may want to make a motion to the court to be relieved as counsel because your client has abandoned you. Be careful not to say that the client has abandoned the matter, because the opposition will take that as an admission and seek to have either a judgment against your client or a dismissal of any action your client may have against the opposition.

SEX AND CLIENTS

All jurisdictions have rules that strongly prohibit attorneys from entering into sexual relationships with clients. Specifically, attorneys are prohibited from becoming involved in any sexually predatory conduct with clients. Any sexual relationship may be construed as predatory in later testimony. This can pop up in a disciplinary proceeding, a malpractice action, or in some other legal action.

Keep mind that the same prohibition extends to the paralegals, staff, and others who work under your supervision in
your law firm. One of the biggest humiliations that can ruin
your personal and professional reputation is for you or someone in your firm to be accused of sexual harassment or be
charged as a sexual predator. The prohibition applies to corporate representatives of your client, as well as personal representatives. The cardinal rule to follow is that sex should be
prohibited under all circumstances.

The rule against having sexual relations with clients applies
to employees, staff, and other attorneys in the firm as well.
The destructive problems of sexual relationships within the
firm are too obvious and too numerous to demonstrate here.
It is sufficient to say that the rules apply to the people who
work within the firm as well as the clients.

If you hire someone who creates a hostile work environment
by the use of sexual harassment or discriminatory practices,
you will be well-advised to document the incidents, give a
warning, and get rid of that person upon the next violation.
Do so as quickly as you can comply with your jurisdiction's
employment requirements.

ATTORNEY/CLIENT FEE DISPUTES
The relationship between the attorney and client is a very
personal one, and as is the case in many other personal relationships, problems can arise. If the client is difficult and
unruly, you, as a fiduciary, cannot retaliate before termination
of the relationship. The attorney must adhere to the standards
of practice, even though the client's behavior is repugnant or
despicable.

You can expect disputes to arise between attorneys and clients, even when you have done everything possible to minimize them. Many jurisdictions have various ways of resolving these, such as mandatory, nonbinding arbitration, mediation, and mentoring. Be prepared to go through these procedures and do your best to extend the most professional courtesies to the client, even though you may not technically represent that client any longer.

When matters have reached that stage, the fees involved in pursuing the money may far outweigh the original debt. You may want to seriously consider compromising the fee. If it is not too large, consider abandoning it as quickly as you can, treating it as a bad debt, and conferring with your tax advisor as to how that may have some tax consequences in your favor.

It is clear that society expects lawyers to adhere to a standard of conduct that is higher than that of ordinary citizens, even if such conduct is not connected to the practice of law. All fifty states have programs that involve attorneys' trust funds, generally known as *Interest on Lawyer Trust Fund Accounts* (IOLTA). Some of these programs require the banks holding trust funds to pay interest on the balances, and that interest is paid to the bar association to be used in helping clients damaged by their attorneys.

CONFLICTS OF INTEREST

Conflicts of interest can be defined as a situation in which an attorney has interests adverse to the client, and the exercise of those interests does some injury to the client. Most of the time, this kind of conflict arises when the attorney has obtained some information about the client, and this potentially could be adverse to the client's interest. The opportunities for those things to happen clearly arise when the attorney and the client are in business together.

The *Rules of Ethics*, pertaining to attorneys in most jurisdictions, prohibit the partnership between attorneys and non-attorneys, and specifically do not permit the splitting of fees with attorneys and non-attorneys. An attorney has a duty to preserve client confidences, and it lasts for the lifetime of the parties involved. It survives the termination of the attorney/client relationship and continues after the death of the client. Only the client can waive the attorney/client privilege.

Necessarily, if the client is dead, the privilege can then never be waived. The duty to maintain that confidentiality is involved and the conflict of interest rules prohibit an attorney from obtaining any advantage whatsoever from that confidential information to use to the attorney's benefit or that of another client.

In order to represent a current client against a former client, if the confidential information is pertinent, a detailed and informed written consent of the former client is required. It is the best practice to have the former client receive independent legal advice as to any waiver of conflict.

The attorney must exercise utmost loyalty to the client, and that loyalty exists through the entire attorney/client relationship. The duty of the lawyer will end at the termination of the attorney/client relationship, but the confidentiality of the attorney/client privilege does not end.

If an attorney has a professional relationship with someone who is connected with the client, in any way, and that person has an adverse relationship with the client, the attorney should obtain a similar kind of waiver before continuing to represent the client in order to avoid even the semblance of a conflict. Such conflicts of interest sometimes are very complicated and difficult to sort out, but you cannot avoid resolving each of them, especially in a transactional practice.

The most important factor in such conflict is that the attorney must check with all clients, former and current, to make certain that a representation of any client or prospective client is not a conflict. There are relatively simple systems, even in the manual mode or in the computer mode to establish these conflicts of interest checks. Keeping a list of all clients in the history of the firm will give you the means for making a conflicts check.

Before taking on a client, after you have established yourself, you should run a conflicts check to make certain there are no time bombs ticking away in your file cabinets. Nothing is more devastating than learning midway through a transactional case or on the eve of trial that there is a conflict, and that you have to discontinue representation of the client because no written waiver of conflict is forthcoming. It does not happen often, but once is enough.

Personal Business Deals

The most significant red flag that a lawyer can be faced with is the situation in which either the lawyer or the client wants to go into business with the other. Opportunities for serious conflicts of interest can multiply and can become very serious. Extremely detailed conflict waivers and specific agreements relating to an attorney's business relationship as well as the attorney/client relationship are necessary, because the lawyer is wearing two hats.

One of the most pivotal incidents of disbarment is a result of a business deal that goes sour. The former clients turn on the lawyer and not only sue for malpractice, but report to the state bar such serious things as breach of fiduciary duty, commingling of funds, and failure to notify of such conflicts. The bar has little mercy on lawyers who are not astute enough to try to avoid business relationships with clients, so make certain that the client gets truly independent legal advice before becoming involved in the business relationship in any way whatsoever.

Most jurisdictions have very strict protection for the client entering into a business relationship with the attorney. Before you discuss a business relationship with a client, you should check those protections in your jurisdiction and talk to the ethics hotline in your jurisdiction, or its equivalent, to make certain that you do not get trapped in the morass of such a conflict.

SPECIAL CLIENT SITUATIONS

Many times, clients will come to you with special needs that affect the nature of your representation of them. Minors present the most common problem because they must have an adult acting as a guardian, and ultimately in litigation, a guardian ad litem. Whatever they sign must be countersigned by the guardian ad litem.

Some clients have physical disabilities and need special care in communicating with the lawyer. People who suffer from any kind of speech impairment must be dealt with carefully. Videotaping and audiotaping interviews with people having these problems is advisable. Make certain that severely handicapped clients who visit your office are cared for at all times.

Occasionally, clients will come to you who are quite elderly. They frequently have hearing problems. You must not assume that they are mentally impaired because they have hearing difficulties. They can be intelligent and know exactly what they are doing, as long as they are being given understandable communications. Sometimes people with hearing impairments may not wear hearing aids. Learn immediately what, if anything, is impeding your communication with any client, particularly elderly ones. It is advisable to videotape or audiotape your interview with anyone who has even the slightest hearing problem.

Clients whose primary language is not English present a very special problem to you as legal counsel. Often, people with language issues are very proud of their limited ability to speak English. They will tell you that they understand certain things when they really do not. You are going to have to be especially diplomatic and adept at finding out the degree of understanding that your client may have, and whether or not your client should have an interpreter.

Once again, as with other clients who are difficult to understand, you may want to record the interview with the client with an extreme language problem.

PERSONAL INJURY CASES

The most common contact that people have with lawyers is through personal injury cases. You will be asked to give people advice with respect to what they should do when they are injured. Be very specific that you are not giving them legal advice until you are engaged as their counsel. Nevertheless, you should give them friendly service by telling them to get a lawyer immediately. Next, you should tell them not to discuss with anyone anything whatsoever to do with fault or blame.

If obtaining personal injury clients as a regular part of your practice is desirable, be ethical. There are unscrupulous lawyers who pay money—and hand out stacks of business cards—to tow truck drivers and hospital emergency room staff for personal injury referrals. You may be recommended by anyone—just do not make it blatant payment for referral.

All jurisdictions have prohibitions against *capping*, which is the blatant solicitation of clients on the lawyer's behalf by nonlawyers. Paying people for referrals is the crudest form of solicitation and is prohibited, as is fee-splitting, particularly with nonlawyers. Avoid at all costs these blatant violations of solicitation prohibitions.

On the other hand, referral fees, under certain circumstances, are permitted. For example, if someone comes to you with a catastrophic injury, such as quadriplegia caused by an accident, it may be in the client's best interest for you to engage experienced counsel to collaborate with you, or take the case. You are entitled to a reasonable fee based upon the amount of work that you do that contributes toward the client's benefit.

You may be the recipient of a referral yourself, depending on your specialty, and the referral fee is based upon the reasonable contribution that the referring attorney makes toward the client's benefit. In both situations, be careful to avoid the slightest notion that there is any solicitation or unauthorized fee-splitting taking place.

Once you have accepted a personal injury matter as plaintiff's counsel, you must move quickly and begin work immediately. If you are representing someone who is outside the area where you practice generally, become very familiar with the rules governing your conduct as a plaintiff's lawyer in that jurisdiction. There may be some restrictions regarding making contact with witnesses and others involved. One of the things that you might consider as a first order of business is to contact a private investigator in that area who will be familiar with all the rules of how to begin the investigation of a plaintiff's personal injury case. Even though such an investigator may require a retainer, be prepared to pay it to get the job done quickly, efficiently, and professionally.

When you receive settlement offers, regardless of the amount, they must be conveyed forthwith to your client in writing. The offers conveyed in writing protect you and your client in future disputes as to whether or not the client had the opportunity to accept or reject a settlement offer.

When your client is a minor, always remember to make certain that a guardian ad litem is appointed by the court before any action is filed. Make certain that in all transactions where signatures are required, the minor's guardian is at least a cosigner.

Under certain circumstances where the guardian is the parent, and there are conflicting legal and financial interests between the minor and the parent, the minor should receive advice from independent legal counsel. Conflicts can be waived in writing; however, a minor may not have the capacity to make that decision without independent legal advice.

It is your duty as legal counsel to explain the basis for any conflict and the reason for your recommendation that they seek independent legal advice. It is not enough to say, "there are conflicts, so get an independent counsel's advice."

CRIMINAL CASES

Friends and family may contact you because they are in trouble with law enforcement. They may be calling you from an accident scene or from a local jail. With cell phone availability becoming so widespread, you can expect such a phone call from anyplace at any time.

When anyone contacts you with a question involving law enforcement, your first comment to them should be that they are to speak to no law enforcement agency or personnel about any facts of the matter until they have an opportunity to talk to a lawyer.

The wish to speak to legal counsel is inadmissible at trial under normal circumstances, and everyone has the right to avoid making statements that can be used adversely at trial. Every lawyer should have some information about a bail bondsman to take care of situations in which clients, family, friends, or others call and need to be released.

Except under extremely rare circumstances, do not pay the fee for posting bail. This is up to the individual person or the person's family or friends. When you as a lawyer get too deeply involved in the financing of bail, it makes it difficult to negotiate your fees.

Unless you plan to develop a criminal defense practice, you may not have a network of people to recommend as counsel. You should have a criminal lawyer to whom you can recommend people when your family, friends, and others need criminal defense counsel. You should give the above suggestions to those people who call you only because they may not be able to reach the criminal lawyer you have in mind.

If you are the source of such referrals, you should allow the criminal defense lawyer to take you to lunch every now and then to discuss the course of events in the case. This also strengthens the relationship between the two of you for future mutual help. Referrals can go both ways, and your services should be understood and available to the criminal defense lawyer if the opportunity arises to refer cases to you.

The following checklist can apply to criminal as well as civil cases. It is a brief primer for the inexperienced lawyer and a refresher for the experienced one. By preparing for the details and knowing the rules, especially the *local rules* applying to that court room, you show respect to the judge deciding your case. Such subtle indicators result in positive results in many ways in court.

Court Appearances Checklist

❏ Go to the courthouse if you have not been there before on other business, and go with your witnesses specifically to the courtroom where you will be appearing. This will familiarize everyone with the surroundings and you will be more relaxed.

❏ Go to the courtroom where you will be appearing at a time when you can speak with the court personnel in a relaxed atmosphere.

❏ Determine the local rules of that courtroom and the court's individual requirements for what is expected of you.

❏ If possible, visit the courtroom while another matter is being heard in order to gauge the nature of the judge and the degree of formality required in that setting.

❏ Always be familiar with the local rules of the courts, particularly procedural requirements, such as where the court requires you to be when you address it. Federal court is very formal.

❏ Always address the court as, "Your Honor," never "Judge."

❏ Always stand when addressing the court.

❏ Always stand when addressing a jury in jury selection, opening statement, or final argument. You may wish to use a lectern.

❏ Always ask the court's permission to approach a witness on the witness stand until the court advises you that it is not necessary to do so.

❏ Rehearse or practice any lengthy oral presentations to be made to the court.

chapter seventeen:
Preventing
Malpractice Suits

While some portion of your legal practice may be devoted to defending your clients' interests in malpractice suits, today's legal practitioners must also remain watchful for malpractice claims against themselves. As the numbers of suits and settlements increase, the affordability of insurance decreases. Lawyers' time and resources are engaged more and more in the resolution of complaints and claims, whether justified or not.

Lawyers targeted by malpractice suits can expect to experience increased stress, anger, frustration, mood changes, irritability, depression, and physical complaints, including headaches and insomnia. These are in addition to the drain on their time and money, and the disruption of their practice. A malpractice suit is a serious event.

Studies of legal malpractice reveal that about half of the suits were brought against real estate and personal injury lawyers. Almost 80% of malpractice suits were brought against lawyers working in a group of five or fewer attorneys, while firms with more than thirty attorneys were targeted in only 2.2% of such suits.

An individual's decision to sue their lawyer—and another lawyer's agreement to defend the individual in that case—is commonly based on the viability of specific complaints. The most common complaints are *professional negligence* and *breach of fiduciary obligations.* However, poor client relations are often cited among the contributing factors in a client's decision to sue.

While the causes of legal and medical malpractice suits may be somewhat different, lawyers and physicians typically are certain of their *rightness* and are often challenged by the necessity of apologies. When conflicts arise, a simple apology may ease tensions and even reduce the possibility of a lawsuit.

THE HEALING VALUE OF "I'M SORRY"

You are late for an appointment. You have kept a client waiting. You have forgotten to return a phone call or send a colleague the documents you promised. So what do you do? Perhaps you act as if nothing had happened—you are a busy professional, after all—or maybe you issue a breezy apology and then act as if nothing had happened.

But who benefits here? Nobody. If you do not mention your lapse, your client or colleague will see you as either scatter-brained or arrogant. If your apology is thoughtless, you will be perceived as insincere. In neither case does the other party feel any better.

The fact is, we all make mistakes. We forget things. We are late. We break promises. Try as we might to keep our lives in order, such lapses are inevitable. Attorneys' lapses can have serious personal and economic consequences—for their clients and for themselves.

Perfectionists by nature, lawyers are trained to be superhuman in order to avoid mistakes. With such high expectations, they may see an apology as not only a bothersome social convention, but also an admission of fallibility. They may also have a tendency to blame *circumstances* or other people rather than admit they have some responsibility for the problem.

While law school training may have included warnings against apologies as actionable admissions of responsibility, studies indicate that apologies are a powerful tool in defusing client anger, restoring respect, and actually reducing the number of complaints that end up in malpractice suits.

Like any skill, apologies require practice. Here are some apology guidelines to start that process.

- *Acknowledge that there is a problem.* Before you can find a solution, you need to admit that there is a problem and begin to define it.
- *Admit to yourself that you may have some responsibility for the problem.* Even if you think you have absolutely no responsibility, an apology may still be in order.
- *Put yourself in the other party's position.* Whether it is a colleague or a client, how are they affected by the problem? Consider how their lives may have been disrupted and how the problem may, in turn, have further repercussions for their work, family, finances, or future.
- *Find out what information the other party needs.* In most cases, people want to know what happened

and why, what the effects and costs will be, and how the problem can be avoided in the future.

- *Do not procrastinate.* The longer you wait to confront the issue, the more of a problem it will be.
- *Make time to apologize.* An effective apology is a conversation, not a speech. Allow time for a complete exchange.
- *Apologize.* If you are able to apologize in person, which is always the best choice, make eye contact. Tell the person you are sorry. Acknowledge that they may have been inconvenienced or damaged by something you did. Explain what happened, but avoid blaming and making excuses. Provide the information the other person needs. Ask for their response.
- *Listen.* Allow the other party to express themselves completely. Especially if they are angry, they may want to go back to the beginning and restate the problem and find blame. Be patient. Avoid being defensive. Again, express your understanding and appreciation for the other party's pain and anger.
- *Avoid interruption.* Do not interrupt the other person while they are talking. Also, arrange a time and place for your conversation where you will not be interrupted by people, phones, or other scheduled commitments.
- *Agree on a solution.* Find something that satisfies everyone involved.

If you have analyzed the problem frankly and you believe you have no responsibility for it, you may also be able to use an apology to express your concern and empathy for the other person. This may have the beneficial effect of making you seem more caring and it may also lead to a productive conversation that will help the person find a solution.

Every contact you have—whether it is with a client, a staff person, another lawyer, a friend, or a family member—is a relationship. Healthy relationships require honesty, nurturing, listening, trust, and mutual respect. Clients who pursue malpractice suits usually cite a lack of respect and empathy as contributing factors in their decision to pursue litigation. Difficult as it may seem, apologizing is a tremendously effective indicator of honesty and respect, and an important step in restoring trust.

REDUCING THE MALPRACTICE RISK

As you establish your law practice, you should be implementing systems and behaviors that will help to reduce your chances of a malpractice suit. Here are some practices to put in place to help in this.

- *Buy insurance.* Many lawyers feel that they are not vulnerable to malpractice suits, so they fail to buy appropriate insurance. This is a mistake. Anyone can be sued, regardless of their specialty, their years in business, or the size of their practice.
- *Be diligent in avoiding conflicts of interest.* Conflicts of interest can arise in litigation as well as when representing multiple parties in a nonlitigation situation, such as estate planning, joint venture, or a small purchase transaction. Attorneys may also be tempted to take equity or management interests as part of a transaction, but these can easily lead to allegations of conflict of interest.

- *Return phone calls.* When clients feel ignored, they are much more likely to feel resentful, angry, and hostile. The failure to return calls is often cited as a contributing factor in malpractice suits.
- *Screen your clients carefully.* You want all the business you can get, but it is important to take the time to evaluate new clients before you accept their case. If a potential client has a history of lawsuits, of firing or speaking badly of their lawyers, or of being turned down by other attorneys, be extremely cautious. Trust your instincts. If you have a bad feeling about a potential client, pay attention.
- *Discuss expectations.* Your clients may have an unclear or unrealistic view of what will happen in the course of your interaction. They may not understand how long things will take or what costs or results should be anticipated. Their expectations may be based on sensational newspaper coverage or television dramatizations. Explain the process clearly before you begin and review the progress regularly as you move forward. Encourage your clients to express their concerns and their acknowledgement during these conversations.
- *Put it in writing.* Expectations and roles should be clarified in writing to assure that both client and lawyer understand their mutual responsibilities. While you may be representing a client on several matters, prepare a separate letter of engagement for each matter. Be as specific as possible in naming the exact scope of your responsibilities in the matter.
- *Deal with mistakes.* Everyone makes mistakes. The worst possible way to deal with a mistake is to

ignore it. Seek advice from experienced advisors and address the matter quickly and clearly with your clients. Apologize with a brief explanation and an appreciation for the client's distress. Provide whatever information the client needs and offer a solution. Ask for his or her feedback and listen carefully to his or her response.

- *Attend to all of your clients.* The demands of a huge case may be pressing, but do not ignore the smaller or more difficult clients. The ones you ignore are the ones that are most likely to sue you.
- *Keep track of deadlines.* The number one cause of legal malpractice is missed deadlines. Make sure you immediately establish a workable calendar system with a fail-safe backup.
- *Keep your billing current.* Establish a billing and collection system that is manageable for you and for your clients. Regular billing is only as effective as your collection system. You need the income to keep your business solvent and you want to avoid withdrawing from cases or suing your clients for nonpayment.
- *Take care of yourself.* You are more vulnerable to malpractice suits if you are unable to manage your work due to stress. Eat regular meals, take breaks, and get some exercise.

In a society where customer service may be the defining difference between two department stores, legal practitioners must pay special attention to the quality of service that they are delivering along with competent client care. Interpersonal difficulties between attorney and client play a large role in client dissatisfaction. With good communication skills, the number of client complaints can be reduced, lessening the likelihood of a malpractice suit.

COMMON MISTAKES

Regardless of the level of your proficiency as a lawyer, there are numerous common mistakes in the business of law. Some of them can lead to embarrassment, some to lost clients, and some to lost careers. Many career catastrophes could have been prevented if the lawyer had admitted his or her mistake as soon as it occurred.

As you establish your law practice and as you continue your career in the years ahead, be particularly aware of these potentially devastating mistakes. You may want to post a copy of this list on your office bulletin board as a reminder. They are listed in order of importance.

1. Not returning phone calls or otherwise being unavailable to clients
2. Not keeping the client updated
3. Conflict of interest
4. Failing to answer the client's questions clearly and without equivocation
5. Failing to communicate a settlement offer
6. Not presenting pros and cons to client before accepting a case
7. Accepting cases outside your area of expertise
8. Missing deadlines
9. Misleading the court
10. Going to court unprepared
11. Failing to advise or seek mediation or arbitration
12. Making unrealistic promises
13. Not keeping up with technology

14. Allowing a professional relationship to turn personal
15. Failing to show respect for clients, staff, etc.
16. Not managing staff
17. Not conducting aggressive discovery
18. Falling behind on billing and collection
19. Not listening to client, cocounsel, judge, etc.
20. Poor time management
21. Not citing sources accurately
22. Blaming the client
23. Blaming the secretary
24. Blaming the system
25. Failing to admit mistakes
26. Typographical errors

chapter eighteen:
Balancing the Scales

From the time you enter law school, your chosen career exposes you to the brutal pressures of expectations, debt, and stress. The more responsibility you accept, the greater the pressures. Many lawyers discover that it takes years to master these challenges and actually enjoy their work and their life.

Deciding on a career in law does not have to be a prescription for unhappiness. You can begin shaping your personal and professional satisfaction right now. Along with your studies of ethics, torts, and mediation, you simply need to learn and apply the tools of stress management. This chapter provides the information you need to identify and manage the stresses in your life and to have a more meaningful, satisfying career.

KEEPING AN EYE ON THE GOAL

Perhaps you have known since age six that you wanted to be an attorney and never departed from that goal. Maybe career expectations were bestowed on you by your family along with your name, or you may have come to your choice later, having tried other professions.

However you arrived at the law, you will ultimately measure your success by the achievement of goals. While timely loan, car, and rent payments may seem to be the only real concern, your professional goals are probably more fundamental and complex. In order to manage your career, you have to keep an eye on why you are here.

The first step in stress management is to identify your goals. Prioritize your goals according to their current importance to you. The following list gives some possible goals you may have.

- *Autonomy:* to be able to determine the course of your work—and the management of your time—with minimal interference.
- *Desirable Location:* to work in a specific geographic area or to have control of the amount of travel required by your job.
- *Financial Reward:* to provide for your personal security through substantial salary and job benefits.
- *Intellectual Stimulation:* to be engaged in work that challenges you or to work among creative individuals who expand the boundaries of your profession.
- *Job Security:* the certainty that your job will be available to you for as long as you want it.
- *Leisure Time:* to have time away from your job to pursue other activities.
- *Personal Growth:* to gain a sense of accomplishment through the personal development achieved in your job.
- *Person-to-Person Contact:* to spend most of your working hours interacting with other people.
- *Power:* to hold a position of influence and authority.

- *Professional Recognition:* to achieve recognition by your peers or the public for your professional accomplishments.
- *Social Service:* to engage in work that benefits individuals, the community, society, or the world.
- *Variety:* to have frequently changing tasks, people, or settings within your job.

Understanding your goals allows you to set additional priorities, create timelines, and make compromises—all steps in the management of stress. Your priorities may change, so set a time each year, such as your birthday, to reconsider and reorder your list. Make sure you are still on the right track and adjust your direction accordingly.

UNDERSTANDING STRESS

Everyone is stressed in one way or another. We live in stressful times. But law professionals experience unique stresses. As time, economics, external controls, difficult people, and social, family, and personal concerns exert their pressures, lawyers are doubly burdened by the emotional and financial demands and expectations of our clients.

When stress becomes incapacitating, it is known as *compassion fatigue* or *burnout.* Because lawyers are subjected to a substantial burden of physical, economic, and emotional stress, they are particularly subject to burnout. The identification, assessment, and reduction of burnout are critical steps in effective personal and practice management.

According to the *Center for Professional Well-Being*, "burnout is a stress syndrome, felt by sufferers as emotional exhaustion." Failure to treat burnout can lead to more serious symptoms and dysfunction. Among the symptoms and expressions of burnout they identify are the following:

- *Somatic*—including exhaustion, insomnia, gastrointestinal disturbances, and rapid breath.
- *Emotional*—including sadness and depressed mood, negativism, decreased creativity, and increased cynicism.
- *Interpersonal*—including quickness to anger, defensiveness, edgy and ready to blame others, and a negative world-view.

Lawyers experiencing burnout may feel *a lack of personal accomplishment* in their work and less commitment to their practice. They may decrease contact with clients and staff, listen less respectfully, be more irritable, order more postponements—and, not surprisingly, provide service that is less satisfactory to their clients.

If untreated, burnout and other complicating conditions may lead to depression and even suicide. Male lawyers are twice as likely to commit suicide as men in the general populations. According to a Johns Hopkins University study, lawyers had the highest rate of depression—nearly four times that of the general population. Approximately one in four lawyers may also feel inadequate and inferior in personal relationships and experience anxiety or social alienation. Research conducted at Campbell University in North Carolina indicated that 11% of the lawyers in that state thought of taking their own life at least once a month. Nationwide estimates indicate that the incidence of substance abuse among lawyers may be nearly double the national average. Substance abusers are ten times more likely to commit suicide.

SEEKING STRESS-REDUCING SOLUTIONS

Stress is every bit as debilitating as any major illness—even for an accomplished, tenured professional. As with other acute diseases, prompt treatment will yield the best results. Here are some suggestions for dealing with this pervasive condition.

- *Recognizing the problem is the first step.* Are you feeling overwhelmed, exhausted, unsympathetic, annoyed, or hopeless? Have your sleeping, eating, or exercise habits changed? Do you tend to blame others when things go wrong? Are you trying to cram several activities into every precious moment? Any combination of these symptoms may indicate excessive stress.

- *Acknowledge that you have choices.* Working long hours in a large firm is only one type of legal career. There are many others, including working in a small firm, teaching law, providing in-house counsel to business, designing or selling legal resources (books, audio tapes, software, etc.), and so on. Your knowledge of the law has many applications. When you find the one that is most suitable to your temperament, you will significantly reduce your stress.

- *Practice coping with criticism.* Criticism—whether it is about your tie or your courtroom performance—can add to your burden of stress, if you let it. Practice your coping skills by admitting to yourself that you are imperfect and you may be wrong sometimes. Then remind yourself of all that you have learned by your past experiences and how good you are at what you do in spite of your past (or future) shortcomings. Repeat as necessary.

- *Exercise your communication skills.* Your stress increases when you are not able to make yourself understood or to communicate effectively with others. Improve your communications by doing one thing at a time, practicing active listening, asking questions, confirming understanding, and following up after meetings and conversations. Even if you are angry or extremely frustrated, avoid blaming, put-downs, generalizations, assumptions, and mixed messages.

- *Remember—you are not alone.* Although attorneys may be reluctant to discuss it openly, stress and burnout are very common in today's multi-tasking world.

- *Nurture your important relationships.* Qualities that contribute to the stability of our long-term relationships are commitment to each other's welfare and happiness; loyalty; admiration and respect; empathy; genuineness; initiative; sharing feelings; and, self-disclosure. None of these will be enough, however, if you do not take the time to be there physically.

- *Apologize.* Apologies are a powerful tool in defusing anger, restoring respect, and actually reducing the number of complaints that end up in malpractice suits. First, admit that there's a problem and recognize that you may have some responsibility for it. Put yourself in the other party's position. Do not procrastinate. Make eye contact. Tell the person you are sorry. Acknowledge that they may have been inconvenienced or damaged by something you did. Explain what happened, but avoid blaming and making excuses. Provide the information the other person needs. Ask for their response. Listen. Avoid being defensive. Do not interrupt. Agree on a solution.

- *Prescribe healthy activities.* If you were your own best friend, what would you recommend? More exercise, more balanced (and relaxed) meals, increased time with family and friends, even having fun! Many people find that meditation, once learned and regularly practiced, provides almost immediate relief for stress.

- *Take some time off.* By the time the problem is advanced enough to recognize, the solution is no longer a quick fix. Although time off seems impossible, you are doing yourself and your clients a disservice by continuing to work once you have reached this point. You will need some time to retrain your mind and body to replace the bad habits with productive, healthful behaviors.

- *Talk with someone.* Seek a compassionate listener—a support group, counselor, clergy, or colleague—who can understand and help you gain perspective on the issues you're facing. The American Bar Association's *Commission on Lawyer Assistance Programs* (CoLAP) offers a variety of services that can help lawyers deal with addictions, depression, and stress-related conditions. CoLAP's mission includes:

> *Education concerning lawyer addiction, depression, and mental health problems, and means of treatment; development and maintenance of a national clearinghouse on lawyer assistance programs and the case law about addiction, depression, and mental health problems; collection of state rules and opinions on*

> *confidentiality and immunity; development of a national network of lawyer assistance programs; models and guidelines for state and local lawyer assistance programs.*

Find out more at **www.abanet.org/legalservices/colap** or call their hotline at 866-LAW-LAPS for confidential local referrals to numbers for lawyer assistance programs.

- *Take time for yourself.* One of the most consistent symptoms of compassion fatigue is lack of personal time. Restoring health means carving out time for yourself—time to read, write letters, go to a movie, take a walk, or do absolutely nothing.

- *Postpone critical decisions.* If possible, put off big life changes for a while. When you are deep in the throes of burnout, the lure of a new job, new spouse, or new motorcycle may seem like the perfect balm. It is not.

- *Step back from complaining and blaming.* If you seem to be surrounded by incompetence, resist the temptation to cast blame on those around you. Consider the possibility that if your life were more balanced, you might be more accepting of others' humanity.

- *Set some limits.* Identify the elements of your life and your practice that are most rewarding and create a living-and-working plan that will allow you to reach those goals. Establish priorities and set limits on your time. Use these guidelines as you make decisions about new commitments and the direction of your life and career.

- *Watch for recurring symptoms.* If you find yourself taking refuge in drugs or alcohol, or experiencing symptoms such as depression, anger, physical distress or reduced self-esteem, break the cycle and pay more attention to your healthful habits.

Your career in law begins long before you accept your first job. It is a commitment that begins the moment you decide to be a lawyer. Effective management of stress should begin at the same time. Even if it means establishing new habits mid-career, the success of your professional life depends upon your health and well-being. It is far easier to establish healthy habits than it is to eliminate bad ones. Start reducing your stress today—your career is in the balance.

chapter nineteen:
A Perspective from Experience

There is no single way to start a law firm. Each person is unique and each factual situation is unique. You may learn from others' experiences how to avoid some of the pitfalls that are likely in the early life of your law firm, but undoubtedly you will have stories of your own to pass along to the younger partners in your practice when you are ready to retire.

The life blood of the firm is clients. Treat them well and you will do well. Answer their phone calls, or if you really cannot, have someone from the firm do so.

Your team, working together, can make all of you a smashing success. Treat them as valued teammates, with respect and a healthy measure of good humor.

Hopefully, you are going to be practicing law successfully for a long, long time. Your reputation will last a long time as well. It will gain momentum the longer you practice, and you should do nothing to cast a negative light on your reputation as a fine, successful lawyer.

Cultivate your reputation in the legal community. It will pay off many times over as you deal with other lawyers. Civility reduces hostility and reduced hostility lowers stress and makes difficult situations more tolerable.

Remember these building blocks for establishing a law firm.
- Communication with clients
- Commitment to clients' interests
- Competence
- Conscientious fees

These four "C's" will remind you of the important simple actions that you have to take to build a law firm.

CLOSING COMMENTS

A law firm is an organization with its own personality, its own culture, and its own future. Your staff wants to make it successful, because if it is, they will prosper. If they feel that they are contributing to that success, and sharing in it through meaningful work, bonuses, raises, or profit sharing, they will be motivated to do the best they can to help the firm succeed.

People are also motivated by effective communication. Praise and positive comments are as valuable as raises and bonuses to motivate people.

Make no mistake—the personality of a company starts at the top, right from the beginning. You set the tone. If you blame others, take all the credit, do not communicate, and fail to meet your commitments, you will soon find yourself surrounded by people who reflect your style. If you are honest, direct, competent, and willing to admit and resolve your mistakes, you will attract other lawyers, staff, and clients with the same qualities.

You may have superhuman expectations of yourself, but you will be sharing your office and your professional life with people who are *just human*. If you honor their humanity, you might find that some of it rubs off on you.

You need to plan and develop your firm's culture from the outset. It is vital for a working team to have a feeling of camaraderie and identity. Attitudes, traditions, and rules are all part of that culture.

Office traditions help to cement working teams. Something as simple as having lunch together on Fridays can reward your staff for their hard work. The celebration of important dates, such as the anniversary of the founding of the firm, birthdays, and holidays can contribute to a shared culture. As the firm grows, you may want to break out the champagne or sparkling apple cider when someone scores a great victory.

There are many ways of showing appreciation. For one of your employees, an extra hour at lunch or a gift certificate at a local restaurant might be more meaningful than a bouquet of flowers. Learn what will be most valued by your staff.

Year-end bonuses and profit sharing are also part of the firm's culture, and these are options that should be seriously considered—even though you may not yet have any permanent employees. An infant firm is like any other infant—it will grow and mature with positive nurturing.

Consistent and predictable management will help your law firm succeed. The people—you in this case—who oversee the organization and its activities must ensure that ground rules are established and followed. That way, everyone knows what is expected of them, and anyone who is working against the rules can be easily identified and appropriate action taken. These rules act as much to provide a model as they do to create consistent behavior throughout the firm. They apply to everyone in the firm. The *boss* is not exempt.

The ground rules establish regular calendar conferences and the mandatory attendance at them. If one or more lawyers or staff members are not required to attend, or are required but do not attend, the whole purpose of the conference is eroded. The ground rules must be enforced or the firm and its clients will suffer. Whether they define the office dress code, office hours, or protocols for indexing files, a firm's ground rules are most actively followed when the staff and the lawyers believe they are evenly applied.

It is the obligation of the founder of the firm to set an example and to communicate to the staff, the other lawyers, and the public the vision that the founder has in mind for the firm. A culture of honesty, hard work, clear communication, and mutual respect will assure that your law firm has rewarding work, happy staff, and satisfied clients for many years to come.

It is the hope of this book that you have a very successful business and a rewarding professional law practice.

appendix:
Resources

In addition to the resources listed below, most law school websites offer a wealth of information on career development.

GENERAL

www.ABAnet.org—The American Bar Association website offers a wealth of information. In particular, the General Practice, Solo, and Small Firm Section will be enormously useful to lawyers starting a new practice. American Bar Association, 321 North Clark Street, Chicago, IL 60610

www.AllLaw.com—Offers a variety of resources, including a listing of national and state bar associations and other legal organizations, articles, forms, and links to journals and periodicals.

www.decisionbooks.com—Publishes books and other career resources for legal professionals and job seekers.

www.gilbertlaw.com—An online bookstore with a variety of study guides, books, audiotapes, employment guides, and practice-specific materials.

www.law.com—Provides legal news and information, including updates on recent decisions, legal blogs, technology information, and much more.

www.lawguru.com—Offers legal resources, forums, searches, and so on, including a well-organized employment section.

www.lawschool.cornell.edu/library/encyclopedia—Cornell Legal Research Encyclopedia is a compilation of United States and International legal resources, including print, microform, CD-ROM, WEST-LAW, LEXIS, and the Internet.

www.lawyers.com—A consumer site that provides listings of lawyers and law firms, as well as a broad spectrum of articles on legal topics, live chat with lawyers, and so on. Information on listing your firm is available on the site.

www.legalethics.com—Offers commentary and links to ethics opinions, government agencies dealing with professional ethics issues, and other Internet resources that address professional ethics.

www.LexisNexis.com—LexisNexis® provides authoritative legal, news, public records and business information; including tax and regulatory publications in online, print or CD-ROM formats. LexisNexis has a new site—**www.lexisone.com/newattorneys**—targeted to new attorneys and small firms.

www.lpig.org—The Law and Policy Institutions Guide is an article database with additional information on significant international treaties, journals, and legal databases ranging from antiquity to the present and representing all nationalities.

http://pacer.psc.uscourts.gov—The PACER Service Center is the Federal Judiciary's centralized registration, billing, and technical support center for electronic access to U.S. District, Bankruptcy, and Appellate court records.

http://store.lawbooks.com—This online bookstore offers Legal Horn Books, Law In A Nutshell series, and dictionaries and reference books. Many also available on audiotape.

JOB SOURCES
www.abanet.org/careercounsel/students.html—The American Bar Association's career counseling site, with links to a variety of resources.

www.bcgsearch.com—BCG Attorney Search is a large search firm dedicated exclusively to placing associates and partners in law firms.

http://careers.findlaw.com—A vast clearinghouse for legal resources on the Internet, the career section of FindLaw.com features listings of law jobs by job type, geographic area, and practice area.

www.lawjobs.com—The job resource center for Law.com, this site allows you to post your résumé, receive job alerts, and search by a variety of criteria.

www.lawyersweeklyjobs.com—A searchable job resource site that lists jobs by position, state, and keywords.

www.vault.com—Job board, list of legal recruiters, and online store with score of Vault Guides, both printable and downloadable.

BOOKS

NOTE: *Some books may also be available as audiotapes or CDs. Check your law library, bookstore, or online resource.*

1001 Ways to Reward Employees, Bob Nelson, Workman Publishing, 2005

Achieving Excellence in the Practice of Law: the Lawyer's Guide with Practice Checklists, 2nd ed., American Law Institute—American Bar Association Committee on Continuing Professional Education, 2000

Ask the Career Counselors: Answers for Lawyers on Their Lives and Life's Work, Kathy Morris, National Book Network, 2004

Attorney and Law Firm Guide to the Business of Law: Planning and Operating for Survival and Growth, Edward Poll, American Bar Association, 2002

Becoming a Lawyer: A Humanistic Perspective on Legal Education and Professionalism, Elizabeth Dworkin, Jack Himmelstein, and Howard Lesniak, West Publishing Company, 1981

Career Opportunities in Law and the Legal Industry, Susan Echaore-McDavid, Facts On File/Checkmark Books, 2002

Careers in Law, 3rd ed., Gary A. Munneke, VGM Career Books, 2004

Collecting Your Fee: Getting Paid From Intake to Invoice, Edward Poll, American Bar Association, 2003

Choosing Small, Choosing Smart: Job Search Strategies for Lawyers in the Small Firm Market, Donna Gerson, NALP, 2001

The Elements of Legal Writing: A Guide to the Principles of Writing Clear, Concise and Persuasive Legal Documents, Martha Faulk and Irving Mehler, Longman Publishing, 1994

Essential Lawyering Skills: Interviewing, Counseling, Negotiation, and Persuasive Fact Analysis, 2nd ed., Stefan H. Krieger, Aspen Publishing, 2003

Flying Solo: A Survival Guide for the Solo Lawyer, 3rd ed., Deborah Schneider and Gary Belsky, American Bar Association, 2001

Full Disclosure: The New Lawyer's Must-Read Career Guide, 2nd ed., Christen Civiletto Carey, ALM Publishing, 2001

Guerrilla Tactics for Getting the Legal Job of Your Dreams, Kimm Alayne Walton, Harcourt Brace & Co., 1995

How to Go Directly Into Your Own Solo Law Practice and Succeed into the New Millennium and Beyond, Gerald M. Singer, West Group, 2000

How to Start and Build a Law Practice, 5th rev. ed., Jay G. Foonberg, American Bar Association, 2004

Law Office Policy & Procedures Manual, rev. 4th ed., Robert Wert and Howard Hatoff, ed., American Bar Association, 2000

Law Office Procedures Manual for Solos and Small Firms, 3rd ed., Demetrios Dimitriou, American Bar Association, 2005

Lawyerlife: Finding a Life and a Higher Calling in the Practice of Law, Carl Horn, American Bar Association, 2003

The Lawyer's Guide to Marketing Your Practice, 2nd ed., James Durham and Deborah McMurray, eds., American Bar Association, 2004

The Lawyer's Guide to Strategic Planning: Defining, Setting, and Achieving Your Firm's Goals, Thomas C. Grella and Michael L. Hudkins, ABA Law Practice Management Section, 2004

Lawyers on Their Own, A Study of Individual Practitioners in Chicago, Jerome E. Carlin, Rutgers University Press, 1962

The Legal Career Guide: From Law Student to Lawyer, 4th ed., Gary A. Munneke, American Bar Association, 2002

The Legal Career Guru's Guide to the Perfect Legal Resume, Elwood J. Murray, Kilfenora Press, 2000

Making Partner: A Guide for Law Firm Associates, 2nd ed., John R. Sapp, American Bar Association, Law Practice Management Section, 2002

May It Please the Court: The First Amendment, Peter Irons, ed., The New Press, 1997, four cassettes

Nonlegal Careers for Lawyers, 4th ed., Gary A. Munneke, American Bar Association, 2003

Objection Overruled: Overcoming Obstacles in the Lawyer Job Search, Kathy Morris, American Bar Association, 2000

The Official Guide To Legal Specialties: An Insider's Guide To Every Major Practice Area, Lisa L. Abrams, National Association for Law Placement, 2000

Real Resumes for Legal & Paralegal Jobs, Anne McKinney, ed., Prep Publishing, 2004

The Resume.com Guide to Writing Unbeatable Resumes, Warren Simmons and Rose Curtis, McGraw-Hill, 2004

Resumes for Law Careers, 2nd ed., VGM Career Books, 2002

Should You Really be a Lawyer?: The Guide to Smart Career Choices Before, During & After Law School, Deborah Schneider and Gary Belsky, DecisionBooks, 2005

Through the Client's Eyes: New Approaches to Get Clients to Hire You Again and Again, 2nd ed., Henry W. Ewalt, ABA Law Practice Management Section, 2002

What Can You Do With a Law Degree? A Lawyer's Guide to Career Alternatives Inside, Outside & Around the Law, Deborah L. Arron, Niche Press, 1999

What Law School Doesn't Teach You—But You Really Need to Know: Expert Tips & Strategies for Making Your Legal Career a Huge Success, Kimm Alayne Walton, Harcourt Legal & Professional Publications, 2000

What They Don't Teach You in Law School, Schuyler M. Moore, F.B. Rothman, 2001

Your Legal Career, Cliff Ennico, Biennix, 1998, four cassettes

PERSONAL GROWTH BOOKS

Give and Take: The Complete Guide to Negotiating Strategies and Tactics, Chester L. Karrass, Harper Business, 1993

How to Get Your Point Across in 30 Seconds or Less, Milo O. Frank, Pocket Book, 1986

The Power of Now: A Guide to Spiritual Enlightenment, Eckhart Tolle, New World, 1999

The Power of the Pitch/Transform Yourself Into a Persuasive Presenter and Win More Business, Gary Hankins, Dearborn, 2005

The Sedona Method: Your Key to Lasting Happiness, Success, Peace, and Emotional Well-Being, Hale Dwoskin, Sedona Press, 2003

The Successful Principles: How to Get from Where You Are to Where You Want to Be, Jack Canfield, Harper Collins, 2005

Think and Grow Rich, Napoleon Hill, Fawcett Crest, 1960

The Wealthy Spirit: Daily Affirmations for Financial Stress Reduction, Chellie Campbell, Sourcebooks, 2002

Index